GUARDIAN OF A PURE HEART

GUARDIAN OF A PURE HEART

St. Augustine on the Path to Heaven

PATRICIA SODANO IRELAND

ST PAULS

Library of Congress Cataloging-in-Publication Data

Ireland, Patricia Sodano.
Guardian of a pure heart: St. Augustine on the path to heaven / Patricia Sodano Ireland.
   p. cm.
  Includes bibliographical references.
  ISBN 978-0-8189-1281-8
  1. Augustine, Saint, Bishop of Hippo. I. Title.
  BR65.A9I74 2009
  230'.14092—dc22

                               2008033683

Produced and designed in the United States of America by the
Fathers and Brothers of the Society of St. Paul,
2187 Victory Boulevard, Staten Island, New York 10314-6603
as part of their communications apostolate.

ISBN 10: 0-8189-1281-2
ISBN 13: 978-0-8189-1281-8

Printing Information:

Current Printing - first digit   1 2 3 4 5 6 7 8 9 10

Year of Current Printing - first year shown

2009 2010 2011 2012 2013 2014 2015 2016 2017 2018

Table of Contents

Introduction

You stir man to take pleasure in praising You, because
You have made us for Yourself, and our heart is restless
until it rests in You.[1]

This familiar passage from St. Augustine of Hippo's autobiography, the *Confessions*, encapsulates his soteriology in three
movements.* Above all, we are reminded that we belong to God,
alone; humanity is utterly dependent upon God, the source and
summit of being. Secondly, there has occurred a disconnection
between God and humanity, a restlessness which is not stagnat-
ing but implies movement. Ultimately, the peace unknown in this
world is achieved in the next.[2]

In his life and through his work, St. Augustine attempts to
answer the questions implied by these three movements. He addresses the issue of how humanity has fallen from its source. If we
were created in the image and likeness of God, how did it come to
pass that we commence life disfigured? What or who is the means
of our restoration; that is, what is required to effect change? How
does the transformation occur: once and for all, or by degrees?
Once the requirement is satisfied, can we glimpse the Beatific Vi-

---

* Soteriology is the study of salvation, derived from the Greek *soteria* (salvation) and
logos (word). It pertains to the doctrine of salvation; whereby, sinful humanity is
redeemed through the life, suffering, death, and resurrection of Jesus Christ.

sion in this life at least in part? Upon what does our surety of this vision rest?

"Blessed are the pure in heart, for they shall see God." (Mt 5:8, *RSV*) St. Augustine trusts the veracity of Christ's words: Indeed, the pure in heart will be given the power to see God.[3] He calls purifying the heart an "obligation; enlist all your energies for this task; be intent upon this work. What you desire to see is clean; the place from which you wish to see is unclean."[4] How is purity of heart a prerequisite to seeing God? Is purity of heart an extrinsic condition; whereby, God imposes purity on those whom He chooses while withholding purity from the rest? Or, is the relationship between purity of heart and the vision of God organic, that is, those who defile their own hearts through selfish attachment are intrinsically unable to behold the God who is perfect love? Positively expressed, does purification of the heart through single-minded love of God transform the heart in such a way that the reward is received in measure in the present life as the requirement is fulfilled, to be received perfectly in the next?

This book examines the specific nature of the relationship between the requirement (purity of heart) and the reward (Beatific Vision), demonstrating that St. Augustine's soteriology requires a change of one's heart that is true, habitual, lasting, and sanctifying.[5]

Chapter One lays the foundation for St. Augustine's thought through a biographical sketch of the saint in relation to his search for truth and his use of Scripture in this quest. Chapter Two highlights an important distinction between St. Augustine's understanding of human nature with that of Luther, who is employed paradigmatically to represent the consensus of Protestant Reformation thought in this regard; whereby, the organic relationship between the requirement and the reward is precluded in Luther's soteriology and inherent in Augustine's. Chapter Three presents a deeper investigation into the post-lapsarian* will and the need for

---

* The post-lapsarian condition is the state of the soul deprived of grace since the first man, Adam, lapsed from obedience to God in the Garden of Eden.

and possibility of grace for sanctification. I would argue there can be no adequate discussion of purity of heart without a sure footing in St. Augustine's theology of sin, grace, and freedom of the will. Chapter Four examines the faculty of the heart, considered naturally and supernaturally, as well as the heart in relation to faith and the faculties of sight, mind, will, body, and soul. Chapter Five describes purity of heart as a state of being, that is, one's sanctification through detached love, an upright will, the single heart, and finally, spiritual virginity, with the latter being a living, vibrant, foretaste of the Beatific Vision. Chapter Six maps out the means to acquire the pure state of being: God, the Church, Scripture, and the habits of prayer, fasting, and almsgiving. In Chapter Seven, the relationship between the requirement and the reward are discussed in light of the inbreaking of the Beatific Vision in the lives of the pure in heart. The pure in heart are the blessed in the world, their hearts having been intrinsically changed through purification so as to bear God's manifold gifts now, to be fulfilled when they are transported through death into eternal life. St. Augustine also postulates on the heavenly estate.

This investigation is a work of systematic theology;* therefore, I have employed a close reading and analysis of St. Augustine's understanding of the relationship between purity of heart and the vision of God within the wider context of his anthropology and soteriology. The task required penetrating the depths of meaning St. Augustine renders to individual terms and explicating his synthesis of thought. Exegesis** undergirds this theological inquiry in so far as St. Augustine's theology is integrally related to exegesis; there is no Augustinian theology apart from Augustinian exegesis. A detailed search of Latin terms, such as *pur, mens,*

---

* Systematic theology is the study of theology according to a specific theme; hence, the topics covered in this book pertain to the theme: the relationship between purity of heart and the vision of God.

** Exegesis, from the Greek word meaning "explanation," refers to the close reading and critical analysis of specific scriptural texts for the purpose of discovering the original intention of the biblical writer.

mund, cord, found in St. Augustine's writings on this theme, has provided the parameters of this study.

Secondary research on the relationship between purity of heart and the vision of God is limited. Although St. Augustine's works are among the most thoroughly researched, there has been scant investigation into the organic unity between the requirement of a clean heart and the reward of the Beatific Vision. Perhaps this is due in part to the fact that St. Augustine did not devote major works to explicating the beatitude: *"Blessed are the pure in heart, for they shall see God."* He did, however, write at length about the theological significance of purity, the faculty of the heart, and the life of the blessed. Etienne Gilson, in *The Christian Philosophy of St. Augustine,* provides a sustained inquiry into the relationship between the purity of the faculties and perfect sight. Gertrude Gillette points to the unity of the pure heart with the vision of God in a short chapter in *Purity of Heart in Early Ascetic and Monastic Literature,* where she links seeing (the eye) with the heart, forwarding the thesis that the heart which is defiled is incapable of perceiving the heavenly vision. Several fine studies have been undertaken on deification in St. Augustine; however, these do not address the specific problem of the organic relationship between the requirement and the reward according to the parameters of this book. It is my intention to demonstrate the saint's emphasis on humanity's capacity for growth in holiness through purity of heart as a response to God's promise of the Beatific Vision and the requirement for its fulfillment.

Biblical Abbreviations

OLD TESTAMENT

Genesis	Gn	Nehemiah	Ne	Baruch	Ba
Exodus	Ex	Tobit	Tb	Ezekiel	Ezk
Leviticus	Lv	Judith	Jdt	Daniel	Dn
Numbers	Nb	Esther	Est	Hosea	Ho
Deuteronomy	Dt	1 Maccabees	1 M	Joel	Jl
Joshua	Jos	2 Maccabees	2 M	Amos	Am
Judges	Jg	Job	Jb	Obadiah	Ob
Ruth	Rt	Psalms	Ps	Jonah	Jon
1 Samuel	1 S	Proverbs	Pr	Micah	Mi
2 Samuel	2 S	Ecclesiastes	Ec	Nahum	Na
1 Kings	1 K	Song of Songs	Sg	Habakkuk	Hab
2 Kings	2 K	Wisdom	Ws	Zephaniah	Zp
1 Chronicles	1 Ch	Sirach	Si	Haggai	Hg
2 Chronicles	2 Ch	Isaiah	Is	Malachi	Ml
Ezra	Ezr	Jeremiah	Jr	Zechariah	Zc
		Lamentations	Lm		

NEW TESTAMENT

Matthew	Mt	Ephesians	Eph	Hebrews	Heb
Mark	Mk	Philippians	Ph	James	Jm
Luke	Lk	Colossians	Col	1 Peter	1 P
John	Jn	1 Thessalonians	1 Th	2 Peter	2 P
Acts	Ac	2 Thessalonians	2 Th	1 John	1 Jn
Romans	Rm	1 Timothy	1 Tm	2 John	2 Jn
1 Corinthians	1 Cor	2 Timothy	2 Tm	3 John	3 Jn
2 Corinthians	2 Cor	Titus	Tt	Jude	Jude
Galatians	Gal	Philemon	Phm	Revelation	Rv

GUARDIAN OF A PURE HEART

1

Sure Footings for the Restless Heart

BIOGRAPHICAL SKETCH IN RELATION TO THE PROBLEM

A man looking for sure footings is an apt description of Augustine of Hippo. He was born in 354 at Thagaste, at that time a small city of Numidia and a former Donatist* stronghold. Augustine's family was divided religiously. His father, Patricius, was a pagan until his Baptism shortly before his death, while his mother, Monica, was a pious Christian. The young Augustine kept Christianity at bay until once, during a life threatening illness, he asked to be baptized. When the crisis passed, however, he had a change of heart and deferred reception of the sacrament. The spiritual hunger he felt in sickness accompanied him throughout the years, although his hunger would not be satiated until he surrendered himself over to the Catholic Church in adulthood. Augustine expresses his bittersweet regret at the long years of wandering:

> Late have I loved You, beauty so old and so new: late
> have I loved You. And see, You were within and I was

---

* Donatism refers to a fourth century heresy whose adherents believed that the efficaciousness of a sacrament depended upon the holiness of the priest; thus the Donatists maintained that a sacrament would be invalid if offered by a priest in mortal sin. This is contrary to Catholic doctrine which states that the validity of the sacrament does not depend on the sanctity of the priest. Requirements for a valid sacrament are a validly ordained priest, the right intention of the priest, and the proper matter (the element or sign) and form (correct words). Augustine fought against this heresy.

in the external world and sought You there, and in
my unlovely state I plunged into those lovely created
things which You made. You were with me, and I was
not with You.[6]

The young Augustine's quick mind impressed his father,
who decided to prepare him for a forensic career. While Patricius
was earning his son's tuition, the youth spent this period before
embarking on his studies in Carthage in idleness. During this
extended time of relative intellectual laxity, he ceased to exercise
the virtues, as well. He entered into a moral crisis, submerging
any previous Christian inclinations. When he finally arrived in
Carthage, he succumbed to the seductions of the half pagan city:
the hedonism of the arts, the immorality of his fellow students,
the accolades won by his literary achievements, and the lusts of
the flesh. Professionally, he craved the attention of admirers of his
rhetorical skills; privately, he craved satisfaction of the senses, and
in 372, he fathered a son, Adeodatus, with a concubine, a relationship lasting until shortly before his conversion.

By 373, Augustine's intellectual pursuits led him to Manichaeism,* a philosophical system unbridled by faith, rooted in ma-
terialistic dualism.[7] He became a devotee but not an adherent of
Manichaean philosophy; however, by 383 he realized the coarse-
ness of these teachings, the arbitrariness of their scriptures, and
the weakness of their arguments.

In 383 Augustine settled in Milan, Italy, where he assumed
a teaching post in rhetoric. Here, impressed by the homilies of
the city's Catholic bishop, St. Ambrose, he gradually familiarized
himself with Catholic doctrine, immersing himself especially in

---

* Manichaeism teaches the heresy of dualism, which views divinity as possessing the
attributes of both good and evil. This heresy taught that the entire universe was
locked in a fierce battle between two divine powers, a wicked material divinity and
a benevolent spiritual divinity; whereby, the exercise of reason and ascetic practices
were the keys to overcoming evil. This is contrary to Catholic doctrine, which upholds the perfect goodness of the One God in whom no evil can abide.

the study of Scripture.[8] He also became aware of the compatibility of Platonic philosophy with Christian doctrine, specifically its treatment of the relationship between responsibility and freedom in the attainment of the good. Augustine found that philosophy had much to offer in the way of explicating dogma, although he determined that Platonic thought lacked the grace and fullness he sought. A critical deficiency is its location of union with the good in the satiation of intellectual hunger.[9] In the company of faithful, astute, Catholics, he discovered charity to be the locus of the good, and while the intellect has a place of prominence, fulfillment is always a gift of faith — above but not outside of reason — bestowed by the beloved (God). The gift once given can be freely accepted; once accepted, the gift must be *lived*. Augustine was then ready to cleave to the Church, where he found the harmony of freedom and responsibility, faith and life, fulfillment and the good — all he had found wanting in his former philosophical and religious pursuits; thus he was baptized and devoted himself to the study and dissemination of his faith.[10]

SCRIPTURAL FOUNDATION

Augustine's quest for union with God led him to the Bible. The zeal of a convert never left him, and his aim was to lead souls to the Catholic faith. To support him in this daunting task, he drew upon his thorough knowledge of biblical texts. He extrapolated a single word, phrase, or verse, such as Matthew 5:8, from which he attempted to exhaust its meaning by weaving in and out of verses and chapters to form a mosaic of teachings.[11]

Augustine preached and wrote out of his own deep faith, for his ministry and his life were one, filled with prayer, pastoral care and simplicity of life. During his lifetime, he single-mindedly strove to illuminate the minds and hearts of others with the same light God had gifted him. To this end, he used all tools and talents at his disposal, most effectively his writings and homilies.[12]

To read Augustine with clarity is to read him within the context of the biblical canon. The Bible forms the theological parameter of his thought, whether it is politics, philosophy, religion, or the arts. The Catholic Church, as the God-given authority over the biblical canon, rightfully assumes jurisdiction, not only over the sacred, but also the profane.[13] For Augustine, it is a paradox of faith that the authority of the Church is affirmed as fully by the heretics as by the faithful. He writes in the *City of God*:

> [The heretics] profit by their wickedness those true Catholic members of Christ, since God makes a good use even of the wicked, for 'all things work together for good to them that love Him' (Rm 8:28). For all the enemies of the Church, whatever error blinds or malice depraves them, exercises her patience if they receive the power to afflict her corporally; and if they only oppose her by wicked thought, they exercise her wisdom: but at the same time, if these enemies are loved, they exercise her benevolence, or even her beneficence, whether she deals with them by persuasive doctrine or by terrible discipline. And thus the devil, the prince of the impious city, when he stirs up his own vessels against the city of God that sojourns in this world, is permitted to do her no harm. For without doubt the divine providence procures for her both consolation through prosperity, that she may not be broken by adversity, and trial through adversity, that she may not be corrupted by prosperity; and thus each is tempered by the other, as we recognize in the Psalms that voice which arises from no other cause, 'According to the multitude of my griefs in my heart, Thy consolations have delighted my soul' (Ps 94:19). Hence also is that saying of the apostle, 'Rejoice in hope, patient in tribulation' (Rm 12:12).[14]

Acutely aware of the errors of human reason, Augustine reminds his readers of the divinely bestowed primacy of the institution of the Catholic Church, its popes and councils, which stands as the bulwark of truth in ever changing tides of human realities. Appeal to magisterial pronouncements, conciliar decrees, and apostolic and patristic consensus, forms the strategy of attack against his most virulent opponents, notably the Donatists and Pelagians.[15] *

Speaking in continuity with the mind of the Catholic Church and possessed with a full grasp of the Bible, Augustine calls both friend and foe to faith, that is, to a grace-filled life within the bosom of the Church. He depends upon the Bible to uphold and illuminate doctrine. Augustine treats the Bible as a divine book; thus every word is Truth.[16] Further, the Bible is read in the light of Catholic teaching, as the Church determined its canon. Augustine's reverence for the text is evident in his manner of supporting practically every homiletic, pastoral, theological, and polemical point with a biblical citation, not merely as proof-text, but as foundational doctrine. He strives, therefore, to imbue others with this same reverence.[17]

Augustine's exegesis is inseparable from proclamation. The entire canon is treated as the Gospel of Christ, New and Old Testaments alike; thus his hermeneutic** and textual usage can best be described as worship. God the Creator is inseparable from Christ and His Spirit; hence, every inspired word therein points to the fullness of the Trinity and as such is an address, or prayer, to God. To utter Scripture is to bear witness to the Trinity even when one is antagonistic to the Gospel, for the words, themselves, are living, i.e., the Word made flesh.[18]

The Word is fluid, imbued with various senses, or mean-

---

* See Chapter 3 for a detailed explanation of Pelagianism.

** Hermeneutics refers to the interpretation of biblical texts according to certain guidelines or rules which govern the correct rendering of the text's meaning. For Augustine, the hermeneutic which governed his biblical exegesis was his Catholic faith and Catholic doctrine.

ings: Christological, literal, numerological, allegorical, typological, moral, and anagogical.* Augustine, in the tradition of the Patristic Fathers, employs these senses to depict a text's richness of meaning in clear, yet profound ways, so that both simple and erudite minds are able to behold the promises of God in Christ, for every biblical narrative is a miniature representation of salvation history. The Father's Word is the action of His Son; hence, in the Bible, we encounter Christ who is the Church's defense and ground of being.[19] For example, Augustine's weighty *Expositions on the Psalms* is a unified hymn of praise to Christ. On Psalm 3:5, he writes:

> The words, 'I slept, and took rest; and rose, for the Lord will take me up,' lead us to believe that this Psalm is to be understood as in the Person of Christ; for they sound more applicable to the Passion and Resurrection of our Lord, than to that history in which David's flight is described from the face of his rebellious son.[20]

Augustine preaches Christ as the meaning of Scripture in inexhaustible ways through the various senses of the texts: the literal, or plain reading; the numerological, which points to the divinely endowed order of creation and salvation history; the allegorical and typological, which illuminate the hiddenness of God and His salvific purpose in things both familiar and spectacular; the moral sense, which begs the question "What then must we do?"[21] Augustine employs all the senses in his treatment of purity of heart and the vision of God.

Further, Augustine incorporates and expands salient teachings of the Greek philosophers, such as found in the dialogue,

---

* God conveys Himself perfectly in each Word of Scripture. Because human reasoning is imperfect since the Fall, we cannot grasp the Word in Its fullness. However, through the power of the Holy Spirit, we can peel away at the layers of meanings. The senses are these layers.

Hortensius. Thus he provides a familiar intellectual framework for his pagan converts. He utilizes Platonic philosophical categories and demonstrates points of congruence with Catholic teaching on subjects such as the doctrine of the Trinity.[22] On the appropriate use of the inspired thoughts of the philosophers, Augustine writes:

> If those who are called philosophers, and especially the Platonists, have said anything that is true and in harmony with our faith, we are not only not to shrink from it, but to claim it for our own use from those who have unlawful possession of it.... [They contain] liberal instruction which is better adapted to the use of the truth, and some most excellent precepts of morality; and some truths in regard even to the worship of the one God are found among them....
>
> These are their gold and silver, which they did not create themselves, but dug out of the mines of God's providence which are everywhere scattered abroad, and are perversely and unlawfully prostituting to the worship of devils.[23]

As beneficial as the thoughts of some philosophers may be, Augustine does not fail, however, to add the essential difference and insurmountable obstacle between the Greek philosophers and Catholic theologians; i.e., the former elucidate freely from the intellect without recourse to faith, while the latter are compelled to speak from the mind in agreement with the rule of faith.[24]

AUGUSTINE'S HEART

As a convert and eventually a bishop, Augustine was convicted of his duty and mission to lead souls into the Church and thus to the Beatific Vision. By making use of what he believed were inspired pagan writings (especially works of Plotinus and Porphyry) in his own theological formulations, he was able to reach vast numbers. Within this present work, Augustine treats purity of heart and the vision of God in seemingly inexhaustible and diverse ways, helped along the way by his philosophical and rhetorical training, yet he maintains the simplicity of the dogma.[25]

Augustine calls the faithful to the grace-filled life set forth in Scripture and confirmed by the blood of the martyrs; wherein, the faithful approach the perfect image of God by cleaving to Him with a pure heart in single-minded devotion.[26] One's vocation, then, is to ceaselessly offer hymns of praise to the Lord of all, as he so eloquently expresses in his *Confessions*:

> Your words stuck fast in my heart and on all sides I was defended by You. Of Your eternal life I was certain, though I saw it 'in an enigma and as if in a mirror' (1 Cor 13:12). All doubt had been taken from me that there is indestructible substance from which comes all substance. My desire was not to be more certain of You but to be more stable in You.[27]

Heart is more than a physical organ for Augustine. The heart is one's being, inseparable from soul or mind. The condition of one's heart reveals the state of the soul. A heart that is pure is a soul that radiates the Beatific Vision. Such a soul, and no other, attains the vision of God. The relationship between purity of heart and the vision of God is organic, requiring a lasting transformation of the heart corrupted by sin into an unblemished bearer of Divine Life.[28]

According to Augustine, God's free gift of grace is the author and the means of sanctification; therefore, the effects of grace on the soul are manifold. Grace illumines the baseness of the postlapsarian* human condition; whereby, persons seek false satisfac-

---

* The post-lapsarian condition is the state of the soul deprived of grace since the first man, Adam, lapsed from obedience to God in the Garden of Eden.

tion through worldly attachments. Grace also reminds us of our dependency upon God for authentic satisfaction, that is, happiness. God reconciles Himself with humanity through sanctifying grace, made effective through the atoning life, suffering, death, and resurrection of His Son. Grace cleanses human hearts from the contaminants of sensual attachment, the locus of which is pride, and grace restores persons to the pristine image of God.[29]

Grace is freely given, but it does not operate in a vacuum. God has also given human beings free will, which is a reflection of the Creator's freedom. Within the will is a longing for happiness, a goal attained specifically through union with the Supreme Good, God Himself. Unfortunately, because of original sin the will is weak; the mind is flaccid; and the heart is shrunken through concupiscence. The mind confuses temporal goods with the Supreme Good — pleasure with happiness, while the heart lusts after pleasures. The flabby will, then, readily assents to the heart's inordinate desires. Augustine warns that attachment to any good other than the Supreme Good avails nothing towards everlasting happiness. This lesson is difficult to learn, as humanity's imperfect will is encumbered by the burdens of sin and temptation. The will is drawn to lesser goods, and the more closely the will cleaves to these, the farther one falls from the Creator.[30]

The human condition is miserable, but not hopeless. The knowledge of, and desire for, true happiness with which the Creator endowed humanity, remains. Human beings love life, despite our miserable estate, and we seek the means to transform our misery into joy. Our vision of the happy life is sharpened to the degree to which we proximate the Good by the intentions and actions of the will, congruent with a purified heart. The history of our salvation is the story of unconditional love. It is the faithful One's betrothal to a willful lover: a marriage begun in time through the ultimate bloody sacrifice of Christ, the Bridegroom, and consummated in eternity. Providentially, by the grace of this sacred union, as the bride willingly surrenders her will to her Husband's will, she is given a foretaste of the feast to come. Even now the spotless Bridegroom loves the unlovely bride unto radiance, so that at the last, the purified bride will live the Beatific Vision eternally — body and soul.[31] A soul turned towards the Bridegroom resembles her most chaste Spouse, as Augustine puts it, in "a more excellent nature [whereby] the body itself which is earthly, is turned to a more excellent body, that is, to a heavenly body."[32]

Each bending of the will towards the Supreme Good results in the increasing debilitation of human pride. This is the process of purification; whereby, the will possesses a single-minded devotion to God, unencumbered by the desire for self-fulfillment through worldly attachments. In Epistle 171A, Augustine, reflecting on the beatitudes, outlines seven movements of the will towards realizing the beatific vision: (1) fear of the Lord; (2) humility; (3) renunciation of sin; (4) ceaseless prayer for continence; (5) corporal and spiritual works of mercy; (6) death to self and life in God (purity of heart); (7) beatitude:

1. *Fear of the Lord*
   Upon the precepts of God, which we accept in order to behave well, begin to establish your life and morals with religious fear, 'for the beginning of wisdom is the fear of the Lord' (Ps 110:10; Si 1:16; see Pr 1:7, 9:10) where human pride is broken and debilitated.

2. *Humility*
   Next, in a spirit of meek and gentle devotion, do not wrestle with contentious animosity against what you do not yet understand or against what seems to the unskilled mind to be sacred Scripture's self-contradictions and absurdities, nor should you impose your own understanding upon the meaning of the divine books....

3. *Renunciation of Sin*
   When you begin to recognize your human infirmity... how far away from the Lord you have traveled (see 2 Cor 5:6), and

when you come to see 'another law in your members at war with the law of your mind, taking you captive to the law of sin which is in your members,' you will exclaim: 'I am a pathetic man; who will liberate me from this body of death?' (Rm 7:23-24). Then the one who promises liberation 'by the grace of God through our Lord Jesus Christ' (Rm 7:25) will console you in your mourning....

4. *Ceaseless Prayer for Continence*
Desire to fulfill righteousness much more vehemently and fervently than even the pleasures of the flesh are normally desired by wicked men.... Constant prayer should be observed, so that those who hunger and thirst for righteousness would be so fully satisfied that not only would their life not be onerous, but they would also delight in abstaining from every corrupt desire, whether by struggling against their own or by fighting another's, so that divinity could be ascribed to them easily....

5. *Corporal and Spiritual Works of Mercy*
The fifth stage adds the counsel of displaying mercy.... For the gift of mercy is twofold, when recompense (*vindicta*) is granted and generosity (*humanitas*) is shown, two qualities of the Lord united: 'Forgive and you will be forgiven; give and it will be given to you' (Lk 6:37-38). But this work also avails to the cleansing of the heart, so that as far as possible in this life, we might be able to discern the immutable substance of God with the intellect alone.... Hence, the Lord Himself said: 'Give alms and, behold, everything is clean for you' (Lk 11:41).

6. *Death to Self and Life in God*
The sixth stage... consists in the cleansing of the heart itself.... Our works must be done for the purpose of serving men or of relieving bodily needs.... Only when we come by stages to that purity of understanding among the good life, either slowly or rapidly, are we then able to dare to say that the mind can approach the most high and ineffable unity of the Trinity, where

the summit of peace lies. Such a goal is not beyond expectation, since those persons who have been reformed after the image of the *sui generis* Son of God enjoy fully the Paternal immutability. First, then, 'Blessed are the poor in spirit,' where the fear of God is found; then 'blessed are the meek,' with docile devotion; thirdly, 'blessed are those who mourn,' with knowledge of their own infirmity; fourth, 'blessed are those who hunger and thirst for righteousness,' where fortitude for striving tames lust; fifth, 'blessed are the merciful, for God will be merciful to them,' where you are advised to give assistance in order to merit assistance yourself... 'blessed are the pure in heart, for they shall see God' (Mt 5:3-8) where neither pure intellect nor the ability to understand is capable of beholding the Trinity in the slightest degree unless we renounce the pursuit of human praise, even though our deeds are praiseworthy.

7. *Beatitude*
Consequently, we arrive at the seventh stage, to the tranquility of that peace which the world cannot give.[33]

Augustine's placement of purity of heart at the sixth and penultimate stage demonstrates the change which the person undergoes by degrees. The heart that is pure bears the Beatific Vision within itself. This change is organic, such that the person whose heart is contaminated with selfish attachments is intrinsically incapable of beholding the God who is perfect love. The relentless training of the will to act in ways that conform to the image of the Son of God, through the cleansing action of grace, effects a transformation of the heart into a pure receptacle of the Son's own life, that is, He who gives "that peace which the world cannot give."[34]

2

Catholic and Protestant Divergence

FOUNDATIONAL DIFFERENCES [35]

Sanctification in Reformation Protestant* and Catholic theology diverges markedly.[36] The root of this divide is in the nature of the person after the Fall,** and critically, the ramifications for the will. While Catholics and Protestants agree that God's grace, merited by the sacrifice of His Son, washes clean a sin-sick soul, Protestantism precludes the free movement towards grace on the part of the sinner. The Protestant reformers taught that purity of heart does not come by degrees, but at once, yet this absolute cleanliness does not eradicate the self's utter baseness. Holiness and sinfulness coexist, thus the expression of that blessed purity is not fully manifested in this life. In the Protestant construct, then, the possibility of progress towards earthly perfection is precluded. The person is both saved and sinner, pure and defiled. To the reformers' mind, purity is alien because nature is irrevocably defiled. The change is *inorganic*. Essentially, all souls are the same; there is

---

* Reformation Protestantism refers to Protestant beliefs which are rooted in and hold fast to the basic teachings of Martin Luther, with variations according to the slight divergences of subsequent Protestant movements.

** The Fall refers to Adam's fall from the grace of God in the Garden of Eden; whereby, he and all his descendants live in exile from our true home in God, suffering under the weight of sin on our body, soul, will, and mind.

no organic difference between the soul of a great Christian, such as St. Paul and the soul of a despicable sinner, such as Judas. They are different insofar as Christ's grace has blanketed the filth of one and not the other.[37]

Like the Protestant reformers, Augustine credits God's grace with our salvation through Christ's incarnation and atoning sacrifice on the cross. He proclaims:

> 'Truth is sprung out of the earth and justice has looked down from heaven' (Ps 84:12). Truth, eternally existing in the bosom of the Father, has sprung from the earth so that He might exist also in the bosom of a mother.... For whose benefit did such unparalleled greatness come in such lowliness? Certainly for no personal advantage, but definitely for our great good, if only we believe. Arouse yourself, O man; for your God has become man. 'Awake, sleeper, and arise from among the dead, and Christ will enlighten you' (Eph 5:14). For you, I repeat, God has become man. If He had not been born in time, you would have been dead for all eternity. Never would you have been freed from sinful flesh, if He had not taken upon Himself the likeness of sinful flesh. Everlasting misery would have engulfed you, if He had not taken this merciful form. You would not have been restored to life, had He not submitted to your death; you would have fallen, had He not succored you; you would have perished had He not come.[38]

All power of the will to persevere in grace is from God, as well, and God, in His foreknowledge, knows what we *will*.[39] It would seem, then, that there is no argument, when in fact the divide is irreconcilable because of fundamental differences in two teachings: (1) human nature and (2) the freedom of the will after the Fall. For Augustine, human nature does not lose its essential goodness. The soul is corrupted but not wholly destroyed; thus there exists the possibility of true transformation of the heart, not a covering over of evil with good, but a radiant, good heart itself. God's order and wholeness prevail. Holding fast to Catholic tradition, Augustine teaches that a sinner becomes righteous by the grace of Christ; i.e., justification* effects an ontological transformation.** The Protestant reformers, departing from Catholic tradition, deem justification a purely forensic act; whereby, the sinner is declared righteous. Christ's salvific act makes it so without effecting change; thus every faculty crushed by original sin remains so.[40]

The exact opposite is true for Augustine, who argues for a complementarity of graces in the life of the justified sinner. Following grace's efficient cause of the soul's redemption, is the assisting power of grace upon the will, which is severely weakened but not altogether crushed. A vestige of power remains so that the will can act in freedom.[41]

For Catholics, these gifts of grace do not preclude freedom and progress but allow and enable them.[42] While such ambiguity is untenable to the Protestant understanding of forensic justice, Augustine lived comfortably within it, and although those who succeeded him, especially Thomas Aquinas, made great strides to advance definitive doctrinal formulations, a mark of the Catholic Church is her ability to accept the *mystery* of God's providential love. For Augustine, no matter how many strides reason makes in discerning God and His attributes, on this side of Paradise, He remains incomprehensible. Rather than a curse, the mystery of the faith is a blessing, for the greatest mystery is the Eucharist, the

---

*   Justification refers to the action of God's grace on a sinner; whereby he is no longer condemned but made righteous before God. Justification is effected through the life, passion, death, and resurrection of Christ. (See Rm 3:21-28)

**   Ontological refers to one's very being; thus when we speak of Christ's act of justification effecting an ontological change, we mean that Christ not only saved a soul from sin and death but changed the person, himself. As St. Paul says, he is a "new creation."

Body and Blood of Jesus Christ. The inscrutability of God's goodness provides the faithful with inexhaustible graces upon which to
meditate, give thanks, and rejoice.[43]

The sanctified life, for Luther, is not nuanced; that is, he does
not view sanctification as a fluid process of growth with jumps
and starts, back steps and strides. Instead, he determines sanctification to be an either/or proposition for the sinner: Either the
filth of one's sins are exposed, or they are covered over by grace.
Those who are chosen will see God, but the manner in which
they greet Him is understood in opposite ways by the adherents of
Luther and Augustine. According to Luther and the reformers, at
the resurrection of the dead the righteous will rise, but only Christ
will be seen, *contra* Augustine's belief, that at the resurrection of
the dead the righteous will be *transfigured in Christ*.[44] Luther's
teachings on justification and sanctification have decisively shaped
mainline Protestant thought. Although there are doctrinal variations across denominational lines, in the present work, Luther's
formulations are employed paradigmatically to demonstrate the
radical differences between Protestant (Reformation) and Augustinian (Catholic) soteriology.

JUSTIFICATION AND SANCTIFICATION IN LUTHER

> The first and chief article is this, that Jesus Christ, our
> God and Lord, 'was handed over to death for our tres-
> passes and raised for our justification' (Rm 4:25). He
> alone is 'the Lamb of God who takes away the sin of
> the world!' (Jn 1:29).... 'The Lord has laid on Him the
> iniquities of us all' (Is 53:6). 'Since all have sinned…
> they are now justified by His grace as a gift, through
> the redemption that is Christ Jesus… by His blood'
> (Rm 3:23-25).... Inasmuch as this must be believed
> and cannot be obtained or apprehended by any work,
> law or merit, it is clear and certain that such faith alone,

justifies us.... 'For we hold that a person is justified apart from works prescribed by the law' (Rm 3:28); and again, 'It was to prove at the present time that He justifies the one who has faith in Jesus' (Rm 3:26).... Nothing in this article can be given up or compromised.[45]

Luther argues that the atonement is realized in the person and work of Jesus Christ. Human works count for nothing in justification. Efficacious action resides with God, in Christ alone. Original sin devastated human nature, with all semblance of God absent: The will is in bondage, and reason is deceived. The righteousness humanity possesses is alien; it is of God obtained through Christ's obedient sacrifice. Sinners are reconciled with God through Christ; sins are forgiven, and guilt removed. The Holy Spirit moves those condemned by original sin to accept this gift through faith.[46] As righteousness is alien to an annihilated nature, so faith is a *passive* response to what God has already guaranteed. Consequently, faith cannot be ardently desired, although the recipient is moved to accept faith by the stirrings of the Holy Spirit. Faith is generated in those who realize that, without grace, they are held in bondage to sin and death; thus faith begins in contrition and continues to thrive in a contrite heart. Repentance, however, is never part of the forensic act of justification. Luther adds that *if we try to make contrition part of our sanctification, we commit a worse sin.* Love, too, is not intrinsic to faith, as it also is corrupted by sin; thus true love can only be a consequence of faith, as God who is pure love renders us acceptable to Him as His adopted children through grace.[47]

Luther posits that because the will is in bondage to sin, the removal of the guilty sentence through Baptism does not relieve the feeling of guilt. He prays: "Lord God, I am sure that I am holy in Your sight and a servant of Yours. Not through myself, for I feel the guilt of my sin, but through Jesus Christ who has pardoned my sin and who has settled all for me."[48]

Luther views sanctification in two ways: (1) as one with justification in the "regeneration" of the sinful person; (2) the living out of this new life in the Spirit in the world before the parousia.* Regeneration and vivification are two words which can be understood synonymously with justification, signifying new life (righteousness) in Christ; whereby, sinners are acquitted in God's court and made righteous by Christ's perfect obedience. The justified are "set apart" for God to use as He wills. God cleanses us of our iniquity and absolves us of our sin. The justified, however, are not wholly blameless. Luther maintains their sinfulness even after having been acquitted in God's court; thus the "Old Adam" holds fast in spite of the fact that the sin and guilt incurred through original sin have been eradicated by Christ's perfect obedience. The post-redeemed difference is that God does not count transgressions against His adopted children, but counts faith as righteousness. While there may be moral effects in the life of the justified, they are not efficacious for attaining oneness with God. For Luther, there are no redemptive ramifications to sanctified life, as human nature remains wholly incompatible with God. In this vein, Luther denounces the Catholic Church's traditional teaching that the acquisition of virtue with the assistance of grace is demanded, and further, it is the calling of all who would enter into the Beatific Vision.[49]

Luther opines that God looks upon the lives of the justified as holy, living in harmony with the indwelling Spirit despite the sins which the flesh continues to commit. The inner spiritual self where the Holy Spirit dwells, reigns in the wayward will and transforms the corrupt actions of the flesh into good works, or fruits, of the Spirit, while the self remains corrupt. Luther explains the righteous "interpret 'spirit' of the inner man like a good tree which brings forth fruit and 'the flesh' [like] the evil tree which produces evil fruit. But it is better to say that the Holy Spirit makes the tree good, rather than to say that the tree itself is good."[50]

---

* Parousia here refers to Christ's presence with us at His second coming.

Luther interprets sanctification as the regenerative function of justification, manifested in the renewal that takes place in individuals before Christ comes again. This renewal, though, is not efficacious for salvation, and it does not possess a process-like quality causing the justified to become increasingly more holy in this life. Sanctification as renewal is "a blessing of Christ, the mediator, and a work of the Holy Spirit" which accompanies justification, counts sinners as holy before God, and empowers the justified to continue the constant struggle against the flesh. For Luther, then, sanctification is incompatible with the Catholic teaching on the way of perfection as integral to unity with God.[51]

Luther's discussion of humanity's marriage to Christ captures the nature of the relationship between the redeemed person, who is simultaneously justified and sinner, and the regeneration and renewal of grace. Christ, the Bridegroom, assumes the attributes of the bride (sin and death). God chooses the bride (sinful humanity), who assumes the attributes of the Bridegroom (eternal life, holiness). The bride does not relinquish her old ways when she enters into the glory of her Divine Spouse; however, her transgressions are not held against her. She is considered holy and pure in the Bridegroom's sight because she has become one with His flesh through their union, thereby making all His possessions truly her own.[52] The redeemed are both sinful and justified, but the holy fruits of righteousness are apparent in the world. Luther compares the *simul* character of those who have been saved by God to the life of a sick person under the care of God, the doctor.

> Thus in ourselves we are sinners, and yet through faith we are righteous by God's imputation. For we believe He who promises to free us, and in the meantime we strive that sin may not rule over us but that we may withstand it until He takes it from us.... The righteous person is at the same time both a sinner and a righteous man; a sinner in fact, but a righteous man by the sure

imputation and promise of God that He will continue
to deliver him from sin until He has completely cured
him. And thus he has the beginning of righteousness,
so that he continues more and more always to seek it,
yet he realizes that he is always unrighteous.[53]

Luther argues that the holy person does not will to accomplish the good through the acquisition of virtues. Rather, sanctified by the Holy Spirit, the justified *spontaneously* do what is congruent with God's good intention for creation.[54] These are fruits of the Spirit and are divorced from human effort. They stand as a witness to what God, in Christ, has done for us.

Luther forwards the possibility of rewards in this life and the next, but these rewards are gifts and not merits or prizes. Rewards do not blot out suffering, which we undergo for the sake of our sins and for our innocence, but such suffering is never meritorious or participatory for salvation. Rather, suffering is indicative of our separation from God and our condition as *simul iustus et peccator*.[55]

AUGUSTINE'S DIFFERENCE

The post-lapsarian human condition within the context of Augustine's soteriology is examined in Chapter Three. His expositions on nature and grace, sin and forgiveness, and will and freedom serve as the building blocks of a dynamic interpretation of the heart which, contrary to the reformers' understanding, is open to the possibility of its transformation into a pure receptacle of God's own Life —grace. Grace as the prime mover tenderly flames the embers of a love for the Good, long since twisted by the diseases of pride and concupiscence. The will, weakened nearly to the point of death, is not wholly destroyed: "Free will is not taken away because it is assisted, but is assisted in order that it not be taken away."[56]

Through the efficient grace merited by the obedient will of the Son on the cross, the sinner summons the courage to bend the afflicted will towards heaven and responds in freedom to accept God's call to an everlasting, radiant life. The first response is feeble, like a young sapling that, straining to survive its first winter, finds the sun and grows by inches towards it. Aided and empowered by grace, the sapling grows upright into a mighty oak, able to withstand any storm. For Augustine, the tree, itself, is good. Perfect strength occurs over a lifetime; holiness increases through the purging of prideful and lustful attachments to all else but God, who is the perfect Good. The way of perfection is a long and arduous journey begun in sin, and by sin not fully attained in the flesh, yet fulfilled in grace in the life to come.[57] The stranglehold of sin decreases, and grace increases with every inclining of the heart towards God in single-minded devotion. The life of the redeemed, according to Augustine, is not an either/or proposition. For one to attain the Beatific Vision, the heart must bear the vision within itself. Every vestige of the chaos of concupiscence is thrown off, and heart and will are *one*. Augustine addresses God in hope: "Then shall I find stability and solidity in You, in Your truth which imparts form to me."[58]

3

Original Sin, Grace, and Holiness

> I intend to remind myself of my past foulnesses and
> carnal corruptions, not because I love them but so that
> I may love You, my God. It is from love of Your love
> that I make the act of recollection. The recalling of my
> wicked ways is bitter in my memory, but I do it so that
> You may be sweet to me, a sweetness touched by no de-
> ception, a sweetness serene and content. You gathered
> me together from the state of disintegration in which
> I had been fruitlessly divided. I turned from unity in
> You to be lost in multiplicity.[59]

Augustine confesses his sin for his own sake and for the sake
of others. He believes confession reminds us of our utter depen-
dence upon God's "sweetness" (grace). Grace transfigures our
will's perverse leanings and enables us to enter into unity with the
Trinity. In his *Confessions,* Augustine relates a detailed account of
a single sinful act (stealing pears) in order to illuminate both the
fallen and redeemed nature of humanity.

When Augustine was sixteen, he allied himself with a group
of adolescent boys who derived pleasure from wrongdoing. They
reveled in sharing stories of individual misdeeds, and their excite-

ment peaked when they engaged in corporate acts of decadence. Augustine vividly recalls one particularly exhilarating episode with the group involving stealing pears. When he reflects on this incident in later years as a Catholic, he is able to see that the nature of the person, though inherently good as God's creation, is corrupted by sin. He relates the ways in which our mutual longing to know God can be debased so easily by egotistical aspirations; that is, our selfish nature leads us into falsely thinking we can *be* God. He shares his experience of a group's powerful influence on the individual for ill or for good. Regarding his theft, one group's influence was damning; conversely, regarding his conversion, another's was saving.

When he places side by side the consequences of his sin and the effects of God's grace in his life, he detects two wills in conflict with each other: the corrupt will turned away from God and toward self, and the pristine will turned away from self and toward God.[60] He perceives the nothingness of sin and the true being of grace. Through his *Confessions*, he honestly relates a life; i.e., he unsparingly depicts the spiritual life of a human being stained by sin and washed clean by grace, and he prays that all may come to the latter in spite of sin.

Augustine's tale of his theft is at once familiar and compelling. One can easily relate to the feelings which led Augustine to act wrongly and his longing to attain the unattainable; however, it is Augustine's hope that one's familiarity with sin will be replaced by an intimacy with grace. The soul riddled by disease will not remain satisfied to dwell within the corporate experience of perversion, but will strive to travel beyond egotistical feelings into humble *being*. Individual and corporate acts devoid of God's grace are not real, that is, eternally life-sustaining. God's forgiving love graces our lives and refines our will to his, that we may share in His life which is true, good, and everlasting.

How does the will become deformed and pervert our inclinations? Why do we desire to continue in sin, and what is the working of grace which inclines the will to conform our lives to Christ's? A brief look at Augustine's world and the questions and controversies looming over him will shed light into why the issues of original sin and the grace of Christ are primary for Augustine, especially in relation to the transformation of the heart toward the Beatific Vision. Augustine's social location and his actions, emotions and experiences may have influenced his theological concerns, but they did not dictate religious dogma. Rather, his Catholic faith contributed to his understanding of the human condition, both the good and the bad. It was only in retrospect and as a believer, that Augustine was fully cognizant of the importance of his theft and subsequent confession as paradigms for humanity's fallen condition and redemption.[61]

Augustine addressed the faithful and those on the cusp of Catholic belief. His spiritual children lived in a world at spiritual war. He called believers to don the armor of Christ and fight against a world racked by sin, ruled by inimical and diabolical powers, lorded over by the Devil, himself. While Augustine recognized this vast cosmic battle, he stressed the inward struggle of the heart. He argued the battlefield is bloodiest where the soul is in conflict — the heart divided. Satan, as ruler of this passing world, entices us to his side by appealing to our personal desires. While Satan is the lord of our fleshly desires, we cannot blame him entirely for all the ills we suffer. Augustine writes that first and foremost, we must look within ourselves for the root of evil and accept blame, for we welcome the Devil's cunning in our lust to be lords over things and people.[62] The enemy is vanquished only when we relinquish our will over to God's will. When we praise Christ as Lord of all, our selfish desires give way to faithful obedience and trust in His grace to make all things right.

> The nub of the problem was to reject my own will and to desire Yours. But where through so many years was my freedom of will? From what deep and hidden recess

was it called out in a moment? Thereby I submitted
my neck to Your easy yoke and my shoulders to Your
light burden (Mt 11:30), O Christ Jesus my helper and
redeemer of folly. What I once feared to lose was now
a delight to dismiss. You turned them out and entered
to take their place.[63]

The fellowship of the saints in Christ offers the soul the only
available peace and rest in this life. Unending joy and serenity
will follow in God's heavenly kingdom. Peter Brown opines: "Augustine's view of the Christian life is determined by the antithesis
of transience and eternity… he must come with yearning of the
incomplete to be filled, of the transient to gain stability."[64] Augustine professes: "You stir man to take pleasure in praising You,
because You have made us for Yourself, and our heart is restless
until it rests in You."[65]

Although Augustine emphasizes the inner struggle of the
heart, I would argue that his theology is in no way individualistic.
It is precisely by lending philosophical and psychological insights
into the individual person that he points to our common human
identity. Our *unity* in sin paradoxically leads to our *disunity* with
God and each other. Especially in his later works, Augustine
stresses our human craving for unity, which he maintains is obtained solely in the Catholic Church, albeit imperfectly. Brown
asserts that Augustine defines himself within the fellowship of the
Church, living among the *populus Dei*, of the tribe of Israel in the
Davidic line of salvation history.[66]

Augustine discloses the perverted turn he takes in his desire
for unity in the act of stealing pears. He associated with a crowd of
youths bent on immoral living; thus in his desire for acceptance,
he feigned participation in their immoral acts. He feared they
would reject him if they knew how innocent he was at the time.
He eventually succumbed to destruction in order to cement his
relationship with his peers. While he faults the group for their be-

havior and their negative influence on his life, he does not blame his cohorts for his personal action. Instead, he admits his own culpability: "The invisible enemy trampled on me (Ps 55:3) and seduced me because I was in the mood to be seduced."[67] He recalls his willingness to participate in corporate acts of evil.

> The theft itself was a nothing, and for that reason I was the more miserable. Yet had I been alone I would not have done it…. Therefore my love in the act was to be associated with the gang in whose company I did it…. My pleasure was not in the pears; it was in the crime itself, done in association with a sinful group.[68]
>
> Friendship can be a dangerous enemy, a seduction of the mind lying beyond the reach of investigation…. As soon as the words are spoken 'Let us go and do it,' one is ashamed not to be shameless.[69]

CHRIST THE MEDIATOR OF GRACE

Grace, not sin, has the last word. Christ, through the Church, is the mediator of grace in a fallen world, comforting, forgiving, and healing. Peter Brown speaks about her task, recognizing "the nature of the imperfection of man… [as] a profound and permanent dislocation: a *discordia*, a 'tension,' that strove, however perversely, to seek resolution in some balanced whole, in some *concordia*."[70]

Augustine avers that no single person or group is capable of relieving humanity's burden of sin. The resurrected Christ is our only hope for a transfigured life free from sin and its awful consequences. In Christ, we find an everlasting home absent of discord and strife and resplendent with peace and concord.[71] Whereas Augustine established his theft of the pears as a paradigm for humanity's discord and remoteness from God through the craving for transitory things, he also beautifully depicts the oneness we share with God and all the saints when we relinquish our sins and accept Christ's merciful love.

> 'Because Your mercy is more than lives,' (Ps 62:4) see how my life is a distention in several directions. 'Your right hand upheld me' (Ps 17:36; 69:9) in my Lord, the Son of Man who is mediator between You the One and us the many, who live in a multiplicity of distractions by many things; so 'I might apprehend Him in whom also I am apprehended,' (Ph 3:12-14) and leaving behind the old days, I might be gathered to follow the One, 'forgetting the past' and moving not towards those future things which are transitory but to 'the things which are before me,' not stretched out in distraction but extended in reach, not by being pulled apart but by concentration. So I 'pursue the price of high calling' where I 'may hear the voice of praise and contemplate Your delight' (Ps 30:11) and You, Lord, are my consolation. You are my eternal Father, but I am scattered in times whose order I do not understand. The storms of incoherent events tear to pieces my thoughts, the inmost entrails of my soul, until that day when, purified and molten by the fire of Your love, *I flow together to merge with You.*[72]

Augustine's methodology is above all an ecclesiology: He stands within the Catholic Church, where all must reside who long to don the raiment of the resurrected Christ, for the Church alone has been granted the authority and power to proclaim the healing word of God's mercy, grace and love to hearts tormented by sin. No one stands alone: one is either inside or outside the Church. Augustine's awareness of human psychology and biology is evident in his explications of fallen humanity's corporate experience of misery, on the one hand, and redeemed humanity's communal life of joy in faith, on the other. Through allegory and typology, he demonstrates the normative use of Scripture for the Church, revealing the centrality of the text in his identification with the Christian community. Indeed, for Augustine, the Word of God is the Church's life.

IMPURITY OF HEART: ORIGINAL SIN'S ORIGIN

> I inquired what wickedness is, and I did not find a substance but a perversity of will twisted away from the highest substance, You O God, towards inferior things, ejecting its own inner life (Ec 10:10) and swelling with external matter.[73]

Augustine upholds God as immutably good; thus the nature of God's creation is good and right. If we who are created in God's image are particularly good, then who or what is to blame for evil? The goodness of God and our nature in His image precludes laying the blame on these; however, the freedom of our will affords us the choice of conforming to the good or rejecting it. Original sin's origin, therefore, is the will turned away from God. While Augustine does not deem God the cause of evil, he believes God allows evil in such a way that His omnipotence and benevolent mercy will eventually bring forth good out of evil.[74]

Our first parents willed to acquire those things forbidden by God, darkening their hearts to His beneficence; thus they entered into the abyss of sin — the transgression of God's will. Augustine posits that as the children of Adam and Eve, the entire human race inherits their sin. Like our earthly father, Adam, our hearts have become cold, inclining us to refuse to accept God's will for our lives. Instead, we crave our own way. We harbor contempt for God's authority, and we pridefully long for self-aggrandizement. For Augustine, Adam and Eve fell even before succumbing to the serpent's temptation because their hearts, through pride, were already turning away from God and towards their own power and knowledge. They wanted to be as God is, but not reliant upon Him, so as to give glory to themselves. Like them, our sin is present before we act because our heart is stained from the start, leaving us with a will in conformity with our fleshly desires. Consequently, Augustine argues, we deserve to suffer the pain, punishment, and death due to a corrupt will.[75]

> That in Adam's sin an evil will preceded the evil act… and what is the origin of our evil will but pride? For 'pride is the beginning of sin.' (Ec 10:13) And what is pride but the craving for undue exaltation? …when the soul abandons Him to whom it ought to cleave as its end, and becomes a kind of end to itself… its own satisfaction.
>
> And it does so when it falls away from that unchangeable good — which ought to satisfy it more than itself. This falling away is spontaneous…. The devil, then, would not have ensnared man in the open and manifest sin of doing what God had forbidden, had man not already begun to live for himself. It was this that made him listen with pleasure to the words, 'Ye shall be as gods' (Gn 3:5)…. By craving to be more, man becomes less; and by aspiring to be self-sufficing, he fell away from Him who truly suffices him.[76]

Augustine maintains the whole person sinned through Adam, not just the weak body or the weak soul. The will, in body, mind, and spirit, craving to establish humanity as destiny's master, caused our first transgression. We were ripe to believe any and all lies the Devil held out to us if only we could "live according to [ourselves] and not to God."[77] Although Augustine maintains God's foreknowledge of sin, he believes it is not deterministic of the Fall, nor is it deterministic of each person's inevitable sinning.

Rather, Augustine stresses the freedom of the will to either act in humble obedience or in prideful transgression. Free will is given to "know that without it man cannot live rightly."[78]

THE CONSEQUENCES OF ORIGINAL SIN

Original sin's effects seem endless to those who are without faith in God's intervention. Augustine enumerates several of the more serious consequences of the Fall: pride, blasphemy, spiritual fornication, corruption, exile, "inherited culpability," death, murder, the privation of good, lust, shame, ignorance, insatiable desire for decrepit things, mistakes, pain, fear, knowledge of evil, and the will under the heavy yoke of sin. In his *Confessions*, Augustine summarizes these dreadful consequences of the Fall as the will's perverse leaning toward three lusts: pride, pleasure, and curiosity.[79]

Augustine condemns pride as both the primary author and consequence of the Fall. Pride accepts responsibility for the first sin because pride led our first parents to choose to supplant God's authority and dominion with their own. As long as succeeding generations are born in sin, we continue to be plagued by pride. Pride also is responsible for our refusal to accept blame and our eagerness to point an accusatory finger at others for our own wrongdoings. For example, we have tended to lay blame on the serpent, the woman, God's prohibition against the tree, etc. Augustine aligns pride with blasphemy, which turns our transgressions into a curse against God, thus our unholy alliance with the Devil is cemented.[80]

According to Augustine, pride corrupts the soul, blackening the heart, for he writes: "A man makes himself corrupt when he falls away from Him who is the unchanging good, for such a declension from Him is the origin of an evil will."[81] Augustine asserts that our corruption need not be complete. The fact that we are created in God's image comforts us with the assurance that there exists a continuity between nature and grace. However corrupted our body and soul may be our nature remains inviolate. God desires to preserve our holy image through His merciful forgiveness. Augustine, in his autobiographical account of the theft of the pears, invites us to receive God's "sweet" mercy by calling on God's name and remembering, confessing, and repenting of the evil that we have committed.[82]

Augustine compares God to a good physician who restores a weakened and diseased person to health and renewed vigor by arousing the dying heart into radiant health through the salves of love and mercy.

> Nevertheless, make it clear to me, Physician of my most intimate self, that good results from my present undertaking. Stir up the heart when people read and hear the confessions of my past wickedness, which You have forgiven and covered up to grant me happiness in Yourself, transforming my soul by faith and Your sacrament. Prevent their heart from sinking into the sleep of despair and saying 'It is beyond my power.' On the contrary, the heart is aroused in the love of Your mercy and the sweetness of Your grace, by which every weak person is given power, while dependence on grace produces awareness of one's own weakness. Good people are delighted to hear about the past sins of those who have now shed them. The pleasure is not in the evils as such, but that though they were once so, they are not like that now.[83]

Augustine explains how he fell victim to pride through the incident of the stolen pears. His nature's good longing to know and imitate God through humble obedience was usurped by his prideful craving to imitate God in power and might. The youthful Augustine sought honor in his deed and in his companions; whereas, God alone deserves all honor and glory. Pride and ambition of the sort that seized him in his theft of the pears he deems a false imitation of God. Yet, Augustine argues, this false imitation is actually an "acknowledgment" of God's omniscience and omnipotence and a "concession" that truly there is no safe hiding place for a sinner.[84]

The sin-racked heart's lust for pleasure drove Augustine to participate in his friends' transgression. He says he did it all for a "giggle" at the presumption that he and his companions could deceive those who would disapprove of them. He speaks passionately about being overcome with pleasure at the mere thought of carrying out this deception, and his cupidity is heightened by the actual deed. Additionally, his sin is made more despicable because his motivation is base, driven by a lust for pleasure rather than a want of physical necessities, such as food for life's sustenance. He calls both sinner and sin a "nothing"; his crime was gratuitous.[85]

> I had no motive for my wickedness except wickedness itself. It was foul, and I loved it. I loved the self-destruction. I loved my fall, not the object for which I had fallen but my fall itself. My depraved soul leaped down from Your firmament to ruin. I was seeking not to gain anything by shameful means, but shame for its own sake.[86]

The lust, or as he calls it, curiosity, got the better of him. He was curious to know God, and in knowing God to be loved by Him. His sharp mind perceived the marriage of knowing and loving, but his weak will sought knowledge in falsehood and love in an idol. He searched for truth in himself; that is, he let his egotistical desires map out his journey, and as a result, he became lost in ignorance. While Augustine discovers evidence of curiosity warping the will as early as infancy, it is his adolescent curiosity, or rather, youthful pinings, which led to the particular crime of stealing the pears.[87] He committed a crime of the heart.

> The single desire that dominated my search for delight was simply to love and to be loved. But no restraint was imposed by the exchange of mind with mind, which marks the brightly lit pathway of friendship. Clouds of muddy carnal concupiscence filled the air. The bubbling impulses of puberty befogged and obscured my heart so that it could not see the difference between love's serenity and lust's darkness. Confusion of the two things boiled within me. It seized hold of my youthful weakness sweeping me through the precipitous rocks of desire to submerge me in a whirlpool of vice.[88]

We abandon God through sin, according to Augustine; thus we sentence ourselves to dwell in exile from our true home of joy and peace in the Lord. The extent to which one's heart is obscured by sin is the measure of one's distance from God. Augustine assures us, however, that this exile need not be eternal. Through God's grace, by the submission of the will in faith to Him, we experience a foretaste of our heavenly home. St. Paul describes this foretaste as "through a glass darkly," yet ever more clearly as through submission, impediments of the will are burned away. The purged heart lives a saintly life in this world in the face of temptation and in spite of death.[89]

Augustine reminds us that by our inherited sin and acquired sins we deserve the punishments we receive, especially death. Death flows from our knowledge of evil, begotten of our disobedience to God's will; thus the forbidden tree in the Garden of Eden is dubbed the tree of the knowledge of good and evil. Augustine laments that the first bite of its fruit brought this horrific truth: "The discomfort of sickness reveals the pleasure of health. 'They knew,' therefore, 'that they were naked' — naked of that grace which prevented them from being ashamed of bodily nakedness while the law of sin offered no resistance to their mind."[90]

Augustine repeatedly directs our attention to the will which freely chose to fall, and by which we are free to continue falling or to cease our descent. He regrets that through our disobedience, we entered into a detrimental symbiotic relationship with sin, so that now our will inclines towards sin. He derives hope, however, from God's promise to free us from this perversion. Redemption is assured when Christ's grace intervenes, comforting sinners with the certain hope that we will be wholly free in the unity of the Trinity.[91]

SANCTIFYING GRACE

Augustine declares we are incapable of effecting reconciliation with God through our own means, because sin traps us in a vicious cycle of depravity. With the assistance of grace, our corrupted will is restored and inclines our hearts towards the way of reconciliation with Him whom we denied. Grace heals this broken relationship, purifies our hearts, and restores the image of God in us.[92]

The waters of Baptism regenerate our selves poisoned by sin and remove its stain; yet even this cleansing does not liberate us from mortal death. Augustine holds that faith would be superfluous if the resurrection of the dead immediately attended Baptism. Death becomes the victor solely through the righteous death of the sinless Christ in whom no spot or stain can reside. When we die with Christ, death paradoxically becomes the birth canal of new life. Augustine proclaims: "Death… if it be endured for righteousness' sake, it becomes the glory of those who are born again."[93]

Augustine testifies God's love is unconditional; He transforms His wrath into compassion and pity. The Lord is ever merciful and abides with us even as we are punished, and He promises to raise the chosen ones after death to take their place beside His holy angels. God's punishments are for the sinner's benefit: "You fashion pain to be a lesson (LXX Ps 93:20); You 'strike to heal'; You bring death upon us so that we should not die apart from You (Dt 32:39)."[94]

The Trinity accomplishes this feat through the Second Person, who frees us and saves us by His atoning sacrifice on the cross. Augustine regrets his own act of seeking a false god in his admiration of worldly prowess, by which he was easily seduced into wrongdoing through the encouragement and accolades of his friends. He says he was able to approach God and turn away from the seductive pleasures and fleeting powers of this world only when he "embraced 'the mediator between God and man, the man Christ Jesus' (1 Tm 2:5)."[95] Christ taught him the paradoxical truth that authentic greatness resides in weakness, for out of the decay of suffering and death emerged the strength of unending life. Christ's rising from the dead is concrete proof that God's chosen ones are saved. We come to the Father through the Son, and the Holy Spirit places the gift of grace, that is, the life of the Trinity, in our hearts. Once grace embraces us, our hearts overflow with joy, not resentment, for being utterly dependent upon God. We do not run to be free *from* His grace but free *for* His service.[96] Augustine contrasts the truly happy life of those who have chained their hearts to Christ in a slavery of liberation, with the phantom happiness of those who choose to wear the manacles of external things.

> There is a delight which is given not to the wicked (Is 43:22), but to those who worship You for no reward save the joy that You Yourself are to them. That is the authentic happy life, to set one's joy on You, grounded in You and caused by You. That is the real thing, and there is no other. Those who think that the happy life is found elsewhere, pursue another joy and not the true

one. Nevertheless their will remains drawn towards some image of the true joy.[97]

Augustine proclaims that the grace of Christ justifies us and removes the binding nature of our guilt. The sacrament of Baptism, by communicating Christ's death to us, brings us life, forgiveness, and the means of salvation. Our new life involves a bending of our wills away from our selves and toward God, the effects of which last a lifetime. Through Baptism, one is empowered for the lifelong struggle of the "old" Adam, whose residual concupiscence battles for the heart's affections at every turn. By the waters of regeneration, the baptized can turn to God in prayer, confess sins and beg forgiveness, confident in God's attentiveness to the heartfelt supplications of His own.[98]

Children, as well as adults, benefit from Baptism, because even as infants and youth we make our first parents' sin our own. Although Augustine writes that infants are not developmentally ready to follow Christ's example in their lives, they may grow in His grace and love as they mature.[99] The example of Christian witness set by children's caregivers goes a long way to remind the young of the gifts they received in Baptism. Throughout his *Confessions*, Augustine praises God for sending his mother, Monica, to abide with him and pray for him throughout his wayward life. Augustine stresses the importance of the Christian community in an individual's conversion. Just as "the group" can lead one into sin, such as his adolescent clique enticed him to steal, so another kind of association can lead one to Christ. Augustine fondly remembers that every positive step his will took along the road to his conversion was in the company of believers. Indeed, he is convinced that to be a Christian is to live, not for oneself, but for the sake of God and His people (i.e., the neighbor).[100]

Augustine's Response to Pelagianism

Augustine's role in the Pelagian controversy compelled him to write volumes concerning humanity's culpability for sin and the necessity of God's grace to lift sin's burden of a heart inclined towards sin, into a heart single-mindedly devoted to its Redeemer. Simply stated, Augustine lays all the blame for sin and death on every human being and none of the credit for forgiveness and redemption.

Pelagianism is described in two ways. The first is as a philosophical theology which denies both the need for divine grace and the doctrine of the generative transmission of original sin. The second is as an ascetic movement within the Church in the late fourth and early fifth centuries which came to be associated with the British theologian and exegete, Pelagius (and two Pelagians, Rufinus the Syrian and Caelestius). Augustine decries the movement's heretical doctrines, most notably, the doctrines of original sin and the grace of Christ.[101]

Original Sin

The heretic Caelestius summarizes the tenets of Pelagianism concerning original sin in his address to the bishop of Carthage. He decrees the old created Adam was destined to die, whether or not he sinned. Furthermore, he denies the "inherited culpability" of sin by postulating that all people are born in the same pre-sin condition as our first parents; thus we may lead sinless lives in this world without benefit of another's aid, and he points to some who he believes led spotless lives. Augustine inveighs against the notion that death is not a consequence of sin, but a natural transition, rendering superfluous the need of Baptism for salvation. Pelagians view a life of rigoristic discipline as the primary determinant of personal salvation; i.e., we merit the kingdom of God by our moral behavior. Augustine, on the other hand, points to a life of worldly detachment lived through the grace of God as capable of entering the Beatific Vision. He cautions us not to rely on the picture of a disciplined life, for beneath the façade may hide a deceit, a heart deformed by a spirit of attachment to the very act of self-denial.[102]

Caelestius' refutation of the generative transmission of sin angered Augustine. To glean further insight into the disparity between Pelagian and Augustinian beliefs, Gerald Bonner examines the contradictory ways in which each views human psychological development. He contends that the Pelagian denial of inherited sin is largely based on their observations of the adult Christian life, rooted in the philosophy of classic humanism. Here, the goal of education is the maturation of an intelligent adult. Because childhood development is not a consideration, Pelagianism is oblivious to the theological issues inherent in infant Baptism. Since Pelagianism does not maintain Adam's sin as inherited, the transgressions of succeeding generations are explained as resulting from following our first parents' bad example.[103]

Opposing the Pelagian construct of human development, Augustine grounds his approach in his observations of the developing child, in whom he discovers ample evidence supporting the doctrine of inherited sin. According to Augustine, the sole plausible explanation for childhood transgressions is found in the generative transmission of sin. Augustine exemplifies the effects of original sin in his observation of a willful child railing against the admonishment of a benevolent nurse: "At the time of my infancy, I must have acted reprehensibly; but since I could not understand the person who admonished me, neither custom nor reason allowed me to be reprehended."[104]

Augustinian theology, unlike Pelagianism, blames the fall on a completely insidious breach of faith in God which affects succeeding generations and is shockingly transparent in personal, social, and cosmic history. For Augustine, even time is a consequence of sin, as the "distention" of time reflects the "distention" of the spirit from unity in God to multiplicity or division between God and persons. Augustine cries out to God: "You are not scattered but reassemble us. In filling all things, You fill them all with the whole of Yourself."[105] He remembers past sins, such as his adolescent theft, in light of the sin he shares with all humanity, and he offers thanks to God for granting oneness out of multiplicity, that is, for concentrating the heart, mind, and soul, on Him.[106]

The Grace of Christ

Pelagius postulates three faculties by which God's commandments are carried out: "*capacity*, that by which a man is able to be righteous; *volition*, that by which he wills to be righteous; *action*, that by which he actually is righteous."[107] Pelagius esteems capacity as the only faculty within human nature which is given by God and is of God's power; therefore, since it is not our own, we possess it against our will. Capacity, however, is feeble, and its strength lies outside ourselves; thus we require God's grace to assist in the building up of our capacity. Volition and action, on the other hand, are completely our own for they flow forth freely from the will. Augustine concludes that if volition and action are within our own power, and if the capacity which we receive from God is weak, then God's grace ultimately is rendered superfluous for willing and doing good or evil.[108]

Augustine rails against the Pelagian doctrine of faculties, calling the dissociation of human volition and action from God-given capacity to be a leveling of God's divine omnipotence. If capacity is weak in us, then God created our nature weak, but if volition and action are unwavering in strength, they are self-sufficient and need no divine intervention. God, then, does not help us to will or to act, but helps us in the "possibility" of willing and acting; contrariwise, Augustine is adamant that our help is found not within ourselves, but apart. Recollecting his personal transgressions in the *Confessions*, he writes of those times when he was not aware that the soul requires illumination from outside itself, because through sin it was alienated from God's grace. For Augustine, the most horrific aspect of equating our abilities with

God's is the implied culpability of God for evil. He remembers as far back as the transgressions of his youth that he alone was responsible for sin; God "did not make sin in him."[109] In this vein, he inveighs against Pelagius' structure of faculties:

> That we are able to speak (our capacity), is of God... but [according to Pelagius] that we really do a good thing or speak a good word, or think a good thought, proceeds from our own selves. Both God and man are to be praised.... Therefore...just as God is associated with ourselves in praise of good actions, so must He share with us the blame of evil actions. For that capacity with which He has endowed makes us capable alike of good actions and evil actions.[110]

Augustine attributes all authentic power to God: "For it is God that works in you both to will and to perform of His own good pleasure" (Ph 2:13). Our selfish will, not God's will, corrupts us. Augustine is unwavering in his stance that our nature, itself, is good precisely because it is of God in whom no evil can abide.[111] We fall away from God when we confuse the goodness of our nature and the goods we receive with the greatest Good, that is God's divine nature. Simply stated, a heart torn between competing loves is incapable of cleaving to God. Augustine hails the positive aspect of his desire to know and imitate God, but repents of his guilty search for God in base pleasures. Likewise, his desire for community was also good; however, the group he associated with defined themselves externally by the attainment of worldly pleasures, rather than by the spiritual gifts they were given.

> My sin consisted in this, that I sought pleasure, sublimity, and truth not in God but in His creatures, in myself and other created beings. So it was that I plunged into miseries, confusions, and errors. My God, I give thanks to You, my source of sweet delight, and my glo-

ry and my confidence. I thank You for your gifts. Keep
them for me, for in this way You will keep me. The
talents You have given will increase and be perfected,
and I will be with You since it was Your gift to me that
I exist.[112]

Augustine attacks the grace of Pelagianism as false because
its substance is the enlightened mind. The only grace in this construct, then, can be the law and the teaching, by which the mind
can conceive and accommodate right behavior: "God imposed His
commands, so that men might *more easily* accomplish through
grace what they are required to do by their free will."[113] When
grace is given insofar as God's will may *more easily* be done, Augustine concludes, it follows that we can do God's will and resist
Satan without God's grace (although Pelagianism admits that this
becomes a more arduous task in the absence of grace). Augustine
attacks the essence of Pelagian doctrine; whereby, grace is thought
to be merited by right willing and acting, as an addition, rather
than a requisite. Augustine clarifies the Pelagian heresy: "By our
deserving the grace of God and by the help of the Holy Spirit,
more easily are we able to resist the evil spirit... therefore, when
[the heretic] speaks of God's help, he means it only to help us do
what without it we still do."[114]

A doctrine of grace that is grounded in commandment-keep-
ing and teaching, and is merited by applying one's own efforts
with or without God, contradicts Augustine's understanding of
apostolic teaching. It is only as we realize our guilt for our disobedience, that we are driven to our knees in adoration and supplication to God to deliver us from our sins and enable us to reverse
our evil ways. Through original sin, it is as if our hearts have been
hardened by an icy blast: Only Divine Love can melt our hearts,
as with grace all things are possible.[115]

Augustine condemns Pelagianism for its insistence on the
meritorious nature of our deeds apart from the assistance of grace;
furthermore, he inveighs against the heresy which conceives of

the will as strong on its own, capable of driving us to seek God without God. Accordingly, God's power has little or nothing to do with faith; rather, it is what we generate on our own that is deserving of grace. For Augustine, this is anathema: Such grace is no grace at all. Grace, as its name bespeaks, is God's *gratuitous* gift.[116]

RECAPITULATION

Before turning to the next chapter, which examines the faculty of the post-lapsarian heart, let us summarize Augustine's teachings on original sin and grace. Above all, Augustine states unequivocally that he preaches a Catholic doctrine that is biblical, apostolic, and traditional. As a bishop of the Church, he perceives his special role as defender of the faith for believers and against heretics. He battles many heresies during his lifetime, but in relation to original sin and grace, his criticisms are most forcefully directed against the tenets of Pelagianism. Augustine holds human nature to be good as created by God; however, nature is corrupted, albeit not entirely, through the free fall of the will. This corruption is seminally transmitted to the descendants of Adam, the effect of which is experienced in a perverse inclination of the will towards sin. Humanity's common experience of concupiscence is evidence of the existence of original sin. Particularly in the *Confessions*, Augustine examines his personal transgressions in light of this sin; thus he views his theft of the pears at a tender age as a paradigm for human sinfulness.

Augustine seeks freedom from the manacles of original sin in the grace of Christ. Grace is opposite in character and substance to the human lusts which previously controlled his affections and drove his actions. Augustine teaches that we receive grace through Christ's acts of complete renunciation of worldly desires, including the desire for life, and Augustine is personally driven to his knees by the contemplation of Christ's ultimate renunciation: the sacrifice of His life for us that we may live eternally. The baptized are called to follow Christ's way of holy detachment for His own sake.

Augustine paradigmatically exposes the decadence of sin in his narration of the stolen pears incident of his youth. He contrasts the baseness of his adolescent sin-corrupted desires directed towards accomplishing evil, with his later sanctified will directed towards accomplishing good in Christ. Through his autobiography, the *Confessions*, he leads us on a pilgrimage to conversion, and he prays his testimony of sin and forgiveness, disbelief and faith, non-being and being, may illuminate the hope for life-sustaining grace promised by God to cleanse the hearts of sinners.

A brief synthesis of Augustine's poignant confession of faith is found in the *Soliloquies,* where he stands naked before God as a sinner in need of life, forgiveness, and salvation. Cognizant of the frailty of the human condition, he is confident that single-minded devotion to God will reap the Beatific Vision — once beheld is to forever possess.

> God, from whom to be turned away, is to fall
>   To whom to be turned back, is to rise again
>   In whom to abide is to stand firm.
>
> God, from whom to go forth, is to die
>   To whom to return, is to revive
>   In whom to have our dwelling, is to live.
>
> God, whom no one loses, unless deceived
>   Whom no one seeks, unless stirred up
>   Whom no one finds, unless made pure...
>
> Thee alone do I love
> Thee alone I follow
> Thee alone I seek,
> Thee alone am I prepared to serve
>
>   For Thou alone art Lord by a just title
>   Of Thy dominion do I desire to be.[117]

4

Faculty of the Heart

SUPERNATURAL AND NATURAL CONSIDERATIONS

The heart longs for happiness, but it is the heart's desire, Augustine tells us, that unmasks the quality of the soul's hope. Is it a hope in things seen or unseen, temporal or eternal? Augustine repeatedly states the heart's true longing lies in happiness, and the means to this end are loving and being loved.[118] In actuality, the means have been given to us in the perfect love of God for us. The critical question posed to each individual standing before God is whether or not one loves God; that is, has one chosen the only true and necessary means towards happiness? Augustine states a directive: "Embrace love, God, and embrace God by love. It is love itself which unites all the good angels and all the servants of God by the bond of holiness, and unites us and them mutually with ourselves and makes us subject to Him."[119]

When Augustine surveys the fruits of humanity's longings, however, he discerns disordered desires. The goal remains happiness, but the twisting of loves has turned this end away from the everlasting towards the mundane. He writes of humanity's attachment to the world: "Those who seek God by those powers that rule the world, or parts of the world, are taken away and cast far from Him, not by intervals of space, but by diversity of affections, for they seek to walk by outward paths and abandon their own interior things, in the midst of which is God."[120] While the only love that avails for happiness is to love God, the human race has shunned God and cleaved to itself.

Augustine's search for the answer to this devastating condition leads him to the faculty of the heart which, he sees, has become muddied by pride and the accompanying concupiscence. The heart's longing for God has been replaced by the lust to be God; thus the heart turns in on itself and by that act sets its hopes on temporal dreams of a false happiness, leaving death in its wake. Augustine calls us to direct our hearts away from self and towards God through His Son. Cleaving to Him, we become as God created us to be: *one* with God's ceaseless, pure love. Augustine confesses this truth to God. "Without You, what am I to myself but a guide to my own self-destruction? When all is well with me, what am I but an infant sucking Your milk and feeding on You, 'the food that is incorruptible' (Jn 6:27)."[121]

Unfortunately, for the vast throngs of sinners, this lesson comes late. We persist in desperately clutching our deluded, grandiose notions of self-importance; thus we shrink into a lonely abyss, out of love's reach. The longing for happiness, instead of directing our course towards fulfillment, derails us onto a path of concupiscence — trapped in a vicious cycle of lust. Rather than fulfillment, we experience deterioration, a beastly existence.[122]

> For as a snake creeps along not with open steps, but by the most minute movements of its scales, so the slippery movement of falling away [from the good] takes possession of the careless little by little; and while it begins with the perverse desire of becoming like God, it arrives at the likeness of the beasts. Thus it came to be that they who were stripped of their first garment, deserved both their mortality and their garments of skin (Gn 3:21). For the true honor of man is to be the image

and the likeness of God which is preserved only in relation to Him by whom it is impressed. Hence, he clings to God so much the more, less he loves what is his own. But through the desire of proving his own power, man by his own will falls down into himself, as into a sort of center. Since he, therefore, wishes to be like God under no one, then as a punishment he is also driven from the center, which he himself is, into the depths, that is, into those things in which the beasts delight. Therefore, since the likeness to God is his honor, the likeness to the beasts is his disgrace. 'Man placed in honor did not understand; he is compared to senseless beasts, and is become like to them' (Ps 48:13).[123]

From such a base existence, dare we hope to rise? Augustine writes seemingly contradictory prescriptions for hope. In *Christian Combat*, he says: "Let the human race take hope and rediscover its own nature."[124] From hope in "nature" he leaps to hope in Christ in the *City of God*: "Whoever... has Christ in his heart, so that no earthly or temporal things — not even those that are legitimate and allowed — are preferred to Him, has Christ as a foundation."[125] If we, with St. Paul, are *straining upwards* to everlasting happiness, how is it possible for our hope to reside in created nature?[126] Pointedly, what is the relationship between the natural and supernatural in realizing the vision of God? Are they mutually opposed, or are they integrally related?[127]

It is important to remember Augustine's understanding of human nature after the Fall. God created human nature in His image, endowed with free will to conform to that image, which is the creative love of God as it exists in the Trinity. The harmony of loves who is the *One God in Three Persons*, extends to and hallows interpersonal relationships. This extension of the Creator into His creation is *grace* — Divine Life. The created man and woman become one in an eternally life-giving relationship, from which springs a "third," the offspring of their mutual love. With the initial freedom to love, however, came the possibility of falling away from the Creator. Possibility became reality with the fall from grace through pride, the manifestation of love turned into the self and away from the wholly Other. The damage incurred was devastating. With grace gone, human nature is deformed, but it is still *human*, possessing the imprint of God, albeit hardly recognizable.[128] This imprint, though, is not efficacious for the restoration of right loves. In an act of extreme humility, the Second Person of the Blessed Trinity condescends to the baseness of sinful flesh in order to lift us into the Trinity's tender embrace. In His arms, we do not fear death of body or soul. "He who for us is life itself descended here and endured our death and slew it by the abundance of His life."[129]

The chaste love of the Bridegroom washes clean the wanton bride, that no shadows be about her. Chastity cannot abide with unchastity. Through Christ's purifying ardor, He purchases His bride (the Church), for she lacks a dowry, and He brings her to her knees in adoration, contrition of heart, and confession of sins. He is moved to accept the bride's worship, although He has no need of praise. Augustine effuses: "God is unspeakable.... God, although nothing worthy of His greatness can be said of Him, has condescended to accept the worship of men's mouths, and has desired us through the medium of our own words to rejoice in His praise. For it is on this principle that He is called God."[130]

Christ's redemptive love is not forced, but offered freely to be accepted by a humble will, ever so weakened by the Fall, but by grace is strengthened to stretch upwards in sorrowful recognition and longing of what was lost. The stretching is the *passionate* impulse of the faculty of the heart responding to the Passion of the Christ, to which the will assents. The prize is won through the grace of Christ, and it is received through the free assent of the will to the heart's pining for the consummation of love with the Beloved. Augustine effuses: "Then... we shall come and we shall enjoy the one thing; but the one thing will be all things to us.... God will give His glory to us so that we may enjoy it; and the wicked will be taken away that he may not see the glory of God. God Himself will be the entire sufficiency which we shall possess as our own."[131]

Indeed, "the human race [can] take hope and rediscover its own nature," for Augustine quickly sets the condition on nature, that it be one with the crucified Christ. True nature does "not love things temporal, for if it were right to love them, the human nature assumed by the Son of God would have loved them."[132] The faculty of the heart is natural, insofar as it is created, but as it strains forward with bursting love for the supernatural God, it touches the supernatural and is transformed; it is *graced*. The heart, once pierced and enlarged by Divine Love, participates in Divine Life. Augustine cries out to God: "You pierced my heart with the arrow of Your love, and we carried Your words transfixing my innermost being."[133]

The soul is immortal, but immortality does not grant love and beauty, as there is a kind of eternal death the depraved soul experiences which is *less* than nature. This state is a deformity of nature whose ugliness is so wretched that beauty cannot behold it. The heart of one so "covered with darkness" is incapable of bearing the luminescence of grace and suffers its just deserts eternally.[134] Since such a heart beats for its own sake, it is enervated. It succumbs to all manner of temptation to fortify its lifeblood — the accumulation of goods and the satisfaction of lusts — but it is only more debilitated with every object it acquires apart from God. Out of weakness, the heart forms unholy alliances to keep up the façade of enjoyment, but the illusion fades in an instant at the whim of another's ravenous heart. Augustine warns: "Tongues that appear to be offering helpful advice can actually be hostile opponents, and in offering love, may devour us in the way people consume food."[135] Such a heart willingly renounces its God-given nature and in the process loses its soul. Living a lie, the heart will expire. Augustine warns of the dangers of imminent death, but offers a sure remedy this side of eternity.

> 'Return, sinners, to your heart' (Is 46:8 LXX), and adhere to Him who made you. Stand with Him and you will stand fast. Rest in Him and you will be at rest. Where are you going to along rough paths? What is the goal of your journey? The good which you love is from Him. But it is only as it is related to Him that is good and sweet. Otherwise it will justly become bitter; for all that comes from Him is unjustly loved if He has been abandoned.... You seek the happy life where there is not even life.[136]

The heart that is true to its nature according to God's creative intention, experiences beatitude. Such a heart is saturated with the supernatural life of grace. This is the heart of the Catholic Church; those within her share the same lifeblood. The Bride of Christ's grace-filled life is beautiful to behold, whose radiance is seen by her Divine Spouse. Augustine draws us to the love: "By loving we are made beautiful.... How do we become beautiful? By loving the Bridegroom who is infinitely beautiful. The more love increases in you, the more beauty increases; for love itself is the soul's beauty."[137]

God has given us the gift of others to experience a portion of the love among the Trinity. When we love them purely and chastely for God's sake, we love them perfectly, and our hearts are transformed by the Holy Spirit into radiant health and luminous beauty. Augustine depicts the ecstasy of love between him and his mother, Monica, shortly before her death as an ascent to Divine Life. His recollection of their sanctified conversation — their mutual mystical ecstasy — is profoundly moving.

> The conversation led us towards the conclusion that the pleasure of the bodily senses, however delightful in

the radiant light of this physical world, is seen by comparison with the life of eternity to be not even worth considering. Our minds were lifted up by an ardent affection towards eternal being itself. Step by step we climbed beyond all corporeal objects and the heaven itself, where sun, moon, and stars shed light on the earth. We ascended even further by internal reflection and dialogue and wonder at Your words, and we entered into Your own mind. We moved up beyond them so as to attain to the region of inexhaustible abundance where You feed Israel eternally with truth for food. There life is the wisdom by which all creatures come into being, both things which were and which will be. But wisdom itself is not brought into being, but as it was and always will be. Further, in this wisdom there is not past and future, but only being, since it is eternal. For to exist in the past or in the future is no property of the eternal. *And while we talked and panted after it, we touched it in some small degree by a moment of total concentration of the heart.* And we sighed and left behind us 'the first fruits of the Spirit' (Rm 8:23), bound to that higher world, as we returned to the noise of our human speech where a sentence has both a beginning and an ending. But what is to be compared with Your word, Lord of our lives? It dwells in You without growing old and gives renewal to all things.[138]

In the passage above, Augustine illuminates the integral relationship between the natural and the supernatural in the human heart. The heart that acts according to its nature is the heart that conforms to the supernatural, for it is the nature of the heart to "concentrate" on the God who is above nature. Augustine reminds us that the Creator has imprinted His image on human nature, and as a way of leading nature back to Him, God leaves a semblance of Himself in all creation, especially in the filial bond

He established between persons. "As we run over all the works which He has established, we may detect, as it were, His footprints, now more and now less distinct even in those things that are beneath us... yet in ourselves beholding His image, let us, like that younger son of the gospel, come to ourselves, and arise and return to Him from whom by our sin we had departed. There our being will have no death, our knowledge no error, our love no mishap."[139]

Augustine is confident God gives us sanctifying grace necessary for our hearts to cleave to the Creator of nature (rather than His creation), that nature may be raised up and, at the last, become transfigured. Nature and grace will be one; God will be all in all. Again, Augustine recalls his mother's display of such single-minded devotion to God as she neared death. He is in awe of "the courage of the woman (for You had given it to her), and asked whether she were not afraid to leave her body so far from her own town, [she replied:] 'Nothing'... is distant from God, and there is no ground for fear that He may not acknowledge me at the end of the world and raise me up.'"[140]

The Heart and Faith

Integral Relationship

The pure in heart share a common faith, that is, the apostolic faith, allocated in varied measure to the children of God. Faith is unique to each individual, as Augustine cites Christ's words in Matthew's Gospel: "O woman, great is your faith" (Mt 15:28). While there exists the character of particularity to faith, it is not bestowed, nor can it thrive, in isolation. Faith is at once an affair of the heart; it is relational. The paternal bond is the author of faith, as God the Father freely bestows faith through grace, and the filial bond encourages and strengthens faith through the ministrations of the Father's angels and His children.[141]

God leads individuals to the gift of faith in unlimited ways. For the very few it is recognized and accepted once and for all without toil or resistance. For the vast majority, like Augustine, the moment of acceptance comes after a long and perilous upward ascent. Augustine tells of his recognition at an early age of his paradoxical need for God and his willful repulsion at the contemplation of this need. Yet, all around him he is bombarded with evidence of God: knowledge, beauty, filial love, and God's Word in Scripture.[142]

God's Word and His beauty in the world are constants; however, filial love varies in its efficacy according to the faith of the lover. As Augustine nears his own conversion of heart, he perceives the truth or falsity of his loves. The bonds of friendship between him and those who led him into error of thought or action were a sham. On his relationship with Nebridius, he writes that his friendship "was less than a true friendship which is not possible unless you bond together those who cleave to one another by the love which 'is poured into our hearts by the Holy Spirit who is given to us' (Rm 5:5)."[143] On the other hand, the company of the faithful, such as Ambrose, Monica, and Alypius, was sanctified. Hearts such as these are receptacles of truth and insight. As they perceived Augustine's lack, his true friends could lead him to faith in God in ways he would be most receptive. His mother's fervent prayers, her presence, and her relationship with Ambrose were providential for Augustine's conversion. Even these, he says, are gifts from God. He prays: "By the 'faith and spiritual discernment' (Gal 5:5) which [Monica] had from You, she perceived the death which held me, and You heard her, Lord.… How could this vision come to her unless 'Your ears were close to her heart' (Ps 9:38)? You are all-powerful and caring for each one of us as though the only one in Your care, and yet for all as for each individual."[144] The heartfelt petitions of a faithful soul will not go unanswered; God's promises will not fail. Augustine became convinced of this truth as he saw it revealed in the living faith of his mother: "At

[Monica's] faithful breast she held on to [those visions and Your responses], and in her unceasing prayer she as it were presented to You Your bond of promises. For Your mercy is forever (Ps 117:1; 137:8), and You deign to make Yourself a debtor obliged by Your promises to those to whom You forgive all debts."[145]

Gratuitous Gift and Human Assent

Augustine vehemently denounces the Pelagian doctrine of meritorious grace by defending the benevolent character of the Creator. To be less than gracious would be a diminishment of the Godhead; thus the origin of faith must be God's gift, as is the end of faith, that is, the Beatific Vision.[146] While the beginning of faith and final perseverance are in God's hands, He has even more graciously allowed us the freedom to stay the course. As we conform to Him through belief and action, we approach His perfection until at last, purged of all worldly attachments, He becomes our all — God in all. The gift is given; the merits of a life so lived are rewarded; final perseverance is the crown. Within God's salvific will, the grace bestowed at both ends of life is present also along the way, so that even our merits are His gifts. The gifts, however, do not diminish the task to live accordingly. In *Admonition and Grace*, Augustine provides the reader with a treatise on the relationship between freedom of the will to believe and the gift of final perseverance, striking a decisive blow to the Pelagian heresy:

> Since 'the will is prepared by the Lord,' (Pr 8:35-LXX) the prayer of Christ for him could not be in vain. When, therefore, Christ prayed that Peter's faith might not fail, what else did He pray for, except that Peter might have an entirely free, strong, unconquerable, and persevering will to believe? This is the way in which the freedom of the will is defended in harmony with the grace of God, and not against it…. The human will

does not achieve grace through freedom, but rather freedom through grace, and through grace, too, joyous consistency, and invincible strength to persevere.[147]

Seemingly invincible, persevering strength falters when one abandons Christ, for a heart hardened against the faith of Christ is a heart defiled. Augustine confesses his own heart's contamination through pride; whereas, the humility of Christ repulsed him when he listened to God's promise of eternal life. Although Augustine admits he "was already signed with the sign of the cross and seasoned with salt" in his mother's womb, his pride precluded his acceptance of the humiliation yoked with the cross.[148] He contrasted his defiled heart with the pristine quality of his mother's heart, the former incapable of enduring the race and the latter a model of continence. When as a child Augustine was perilously close to dying, he credits Monica's prayers with staving off death while his soul persisted in a damnable state: "With a pure heart and faith in You she even more lovingly travailed in labor for my eternal salvation."[149]

Augustine perceives in his mother the "simple and unaffected faith" which only Christ can give. To be capable of receiving this gift, Augustine realizes that we must accept it as children: We drink pure milk as babes, satiated, without desire for any other nourishment. Satisfied, we begin to develop the virtues out of love for God Himself, and love of our neighbor in Him. By placing ourselves under Him, we are protected from all evil. As we "put Him on" in this life, we experience an internal victory over death, unscathed from external temptations and trials.[150]

The will which submits to Christ performs an act of faith. Faith, declares Augustine, sets us on the path of righteousness, and it steers the course through a determination of the will to master the virtues and overcome vice. Christ gives and receives faith, for it is the love of God in Christ, the partaker of mortal flesh and Mediator between Creator and creature, who accepts a virtuous heart as His own.[151] As eternity dwells in the Son of Man's temporality, so also a mortal being dons the raiment of immortality when by faith in Him one is good in things temporal. Augustine states: "The faith in temporal things, which the Eternal One did and suffered for us in the man whom He bore in time and led to eternal things, is also useful in acquiring those eternal things, and that the virtues themselves, whereby one lives prudently, bravely, temperately, and justly in this temporal mortality, are not true virtues unless they are referred to the same faith which, though temporal, leads, nevertheless to eternal things."[152]

Virtues proceeding from faith possess a divine origin and are thus efficacious towards the cleansing of our hearts; i.e., we are righteous as we live inwardly and outwardly by faith. Sadly, virtues are counted as vice against those who "drag along with us the traces of our mortal nature as derived from Adam," and righteousness and vice cannot abide together.[153] To live unfaithfully is to live without God and so, Augustine laments, is to dwell in darkness, piloting the ship of life on the sea of self-demise. With God, he rejoices, we are as "an infant sucking Your milk and feeding on You, 'the food that is incorruptible' (Jn 6:27)."[154] Out of the depths we cry to the Lord, and He answers, for "nothing is nearer to Your ears than a confessing heart and a life grounded in faith."[155]

Faith and Truth

Faith is adherence of the whole person — body, mind, and spirit — to Truth, the truth of the Trinity and hope of eternal life. Because we are encumbered by the effects of original sin, faith is far removed from the clarity to understand these truths. Augustine cautions us not to be discouraged by our cloudy vision, for we will receive clearer knowledge of truth the more fervently we live out our faith through prayer, as well as exercise virtue within the distention of time. In this way faith works as an astringent, cleansing our hearts to arrive, not merely at the contemplation of truth, but at Truth Itself. Faith becomes truth in a glorious transformation. Augustine effuses: "'Now this is eternal life, that they may know Thee, the only true God, and Him whom Thou has sent, Jesus Christ' (Jn 17:3); when our faith by seeing shall be transformed into truth, then eternity shall hold fast to our own mortality that has then been changed."[156]

We can claim as ours this faith, efficacious for our cleansing, insofar as we disclaim it. The mystery of faith is that we possess it in the selfless act of relinquishing it to its source and summit, God. We do not boast of faith as our accomplishment; rather, we cherish faith as gift and give all credit for its benefits to the Giver. The heart that is pure becomes so supernaturally, by faith in Christ; the heart vanquished by sin becomes invincible by grace.[157]

Faith, Reason, and Belief

> The reader of this treatise on the Trinity should know beforehand that our pen is on the watch for the sophistries of those who consider it beneath their dignity to begin with faith, and who thus are led into error by their immature and perverted love of reason.[158]

The mind, according to Augustine, that seeks after truth without the eye of faith, will necessarily be led astray. Even those pagan philosophers whom he openly admired for their astuteness and from whom he borrowed, lacked in understanding. Worse are those who trade faith for pride in the training of their minds to gain accolades. An examination of their intellectual fruits will discover they are, at bottom, senseless. The confusion of their thoughts invariably leads to a depravity of heart. Those who deny God satisfy their want with corrupt thoughts, words, and deeds.[159]

One can defile the soul by exerting the least amount of effort. Unfortunately, no amount of toil or strain can purify it. Reason without faith compounds the deformation; however, when by reason the problem is determined, reason enlightened by faith perceives the solution. For Augustine, reason is one of our most cherished gifts, for it can compel us to believe what we are unable to see. Once truth is believed, it is understood in measure as God allows. Augustine cries out: "Believe that you may understand."[160] The very act of stretching the mind to grasp what faith believes is an act of faith; it is a drawing nearer of heart and mind to the vision of God. Reason, grounded in faith, leads us to certainty of truth — the certainty that it isn't by reason that we attain freedom, but by faith. Faith surpasses reason, as Augustine argues: "What human reason does not grasp faith lays hold on, and where human reason fails faith succeeds."[161]

Faith surpasses reason but does not negate it. Augustine is a man of reason: Intemperate reason fettered by pride led him into falsehood; reason tempered by a dawning faith drew him to the truth of the Catholic Church. His eyes were opened to the insanity of his former false thinking and the sublime order of Catholicism as he heard it from the lips of the Catholic bishop, Ambrose. The congruence between faith and reason undergirds his teachings.[162]

Faith's cleansing action is the prerequisite of understanding. Etienne Gilson synthesizes Augustine's teachings on faith and reason: "Faith is the heart of the matter. Faith tells us what there is to understand; it purifies the heart, and so allows reason to profit from discussion; it enables reason to arrive at an understanding of God's revelation. When Augustine speaks of understanding, he always has in mind the product of a rational activity for which faith prepares the way, namely that indivisible unity which he calls 'the understanding of faith.'"[163]

Indeed, Augustine determines, in a Catholic's mind, purity of heart is never absent from the exercise of reason; thus reasoning possesses a moral dimension. Augustine's act of submission, by placing reason under the authority of faith, was a moral act involving the whole person. When he surrendered his mind to the dogmas of the Church, he placed his will under the yoke of obedience to its precepts. His fiat was an acceptance of grace's cleansing balm into his heart.[164]

Augustine felt the lifeblood of faith in Christ run through his veins. To be one with Christ, he knew, was to imitate Christ's humility. As Christ was glorified in His act of extreme humiliation, so we, His children, are illuminated in our surrender of self to Him. The whole person must be lucent in order to behold the Light. Etienne Gilson expounds on Augustine's treatment of faith and mind: "Faith is both a purification and illumination. It subjects the soul to that authority whereby 'the lives of the good are easily purified, not through the obscurity of arguments but through the authority of mysteries' (*On Order* 2.9.27); it busies itself with man in order to transform him completely."[165]

The submission of reason to faith leads to the conviction and confession of Christian doctrine and, consequently, the illumination of reason to comprehend what is believed. Augustine reassures us: "Let us hold fast to this rule, that what has not yet become clear to our intellect may still be preserved by the firmness of our faith."[166] Clarity depends on belief. Hold fast to the faith; confess the Creed of the Church. By constant profession of the beliefs contained therein, the Holy Spirit shall convey these essential truths from the lips to the heart. The heart, thereby, infused with Divine charity, becomes a chaste receptacle of Divine Wisdom from which the mind can perceive the truths of God's salvific work: namely Christ incarnate; Christ suffering; Christ crucified; Christ risen from the dead. Heart and mind are thus joined in a spiritual union with the Trinity. Augustine recalls St. Paul's words to the Philippians: "'One thing I do; forgetting what is behind, I strain forward to what is before. I press on in purpose towards the goal of God's heavenly call in Christ Jesus. Let us then, as many as are perfect, be of this mind' (Ph 3:13-15).... the right purpose is that which proceeds from faith."[167]

Since our purpose is to be heaven-bound, we cling to our

other-worldly goal by detaching from all that is earth-bound. We find God by believing eternal truths which we see dimly now, trusting we will obtain full sight when He reveals Himself to us. The conversion of the heart is thus an illumination of the mind. Augustine confesses: "We were converted to You (Ps 50:15), light was created, and suddenly we 'who were once darkness are now light in the Lord' (Eph 5:8)."[168] "Nevertheless we still act on faith, not yet on sight, 'For by hope we have been saved' (2 Cor 5:7)."[169]

Faith and Love

The faith which is efficacious for sight possesses the character of love; faith's fruitfulness depends on love. This is the faith which distinguishes between believers and infidels. When God imprinted His image on our souls, He imprinted love, for God is a relational being. It was for love of sinful humanity that He sacrificed His Son for us, who in turn sacrificed His Life for us. Augustine argues that even the devils believe, but since they have abandoned love, they have lost hope; therefore, those who follow devils have relinquished all hope of the Beatific Vision. While every creature on earth trembles before the sight of God, only the pure in heart trembles with the godly fear of one who hopes for eternal rest. The person who chooses concupiscence for a spouse, trembles with despair over the chaos of eternal death.[170]

Echoing St. Paul's Letter to the Galatians, Augustine tells us that faith working through love effects hope. The trinity of faith, hope, and charity refine the heart for clearer sight. Love is the basis of faith's sure hope in the Beatific Vision, realized afterwards, but glimpsed in this life. Love is also the *form* of faith and hope. Through love, then, faith leads reason into right belief, and hope tempers the will to act in upright ways. Love, itself, transfigures the heart: God's providence loves us into new beings; we respond in kind and *are*. Charity is the supreme gift of God, the pledge and proof that His Holy Spirit is hallowing and cleansing our hearts. While we may groan for the everlasting prize, once sanctified, we groan with hope and we *will* to live in the present as though the prize were in our midst. Indeed, it is, Augustine proclaims, through the Catholic Church.[171]

Faith and the Beatific Vision

The sanctification and the purification of the heart mark the *commencement* of eternal happiness. Faith assures this beginning will have a blessed completion in Truth; thus, Augustine contends, the relationship between faith and truth holds fast. Inscrutably, faith's forward seeking of Truth is a backward gaze on the economy of salvation, preserved and disseminated by the Catholic Church. By believing the mysteries of faith revealed in salvific history, we experience a *foretaste* of the eternally joyful feast to come.[172] He teaches:

> But while we are absent from the Lord and walk by faith and not by sight (2 Cor 5:6-7), we must see the back parts of Christ, namely, His flesh, by the faith itself, that is, we must stand on the solid foundation of the faith which the rock signifies, and gaze upon it from such an impregnable watch-tower, namely, in the Catholic Church, of which it is said: 'and upon this rock I will build my Church' (Mt 16:18). For, the more certainly we love the face of Christ which we desire to see, the more we recognize in His back parts how much Christ has first loved us. The reward of our faith is the resurrection of the body of the Lord.... [Those who] do not believe it in the Catholic Church, but in some schism or heresy, do not see the back parts of the Lord from a place that is near Him.... 'Behold, there is a palace near me, and you shall stand upon the rock?' What

earthly place is near the Lord, if that is not near Him which touches Him spiritually? For what place is not near the Lord, who reaches from end to end mightily, and orders all things sweetly (see Ws 8:1), of whom it is said that Heaven is His throne and the earth His footstool, and who said: 'What house will you build to me, and what place for my rest? Has not my hand made all these things?' (Is 66:1-2). The place near Him, on which one stands upon a rock, is understood to be the Catholic Church itself, where he who believes in His resurrection healthfully sees the Pasch of the Lord, that is, the passing by of the Lord and his back parts, that is, His body. 'And you shall stand upon the rock,' He said, 'when my glory shall pass.'[173]

Faith's backward gaze strengthens the believer's reserve when patience runs thin, trials increase, and temptations of the flesh threaten to squelch hope. Augustine begs his hearers to "be blessed in hope."[174] In other words, believe and love, for faith working through love keeps hope burning bright for the attainment of the object of one's love. Be righteous in action towards self and others; trust in the veracity of the Church; sharpen sight through a spirit of detachment; hold fast to God's merciful will; pray to God who will hear and answer. One who is "blessed in hope" will have no anxiety about the future, "for by patience he expects the blessedness which he does not yet possess."[175] The crowning glory of faith working through love is the contemplation of the Blessed Trinity. Below, Augustine lends brief insight on the meaning of Matthew 5:8: *"Blessed are the pure in heart, for they shall see God."*

Contemplation is indeed the reward of faith, and our hearts are purified by faith in preparation for this reward, as it is written: 'Cleansing their hearts by faith.' But that our hearts will be purified for that contemplation is proved in a very explicit way by this sentence: *'Blessed are the clean of heart for they shall see God.'* And because this is everlasting life God says in the Psalm: 'I will fill him with length of days and I will show him my salvation' (Ps 90:16). Therefore, whether we hear: 'Show us the Son,' or 'Show us the Father,' the one has just as much force as the other, for neither one can be shown without the other. For they are one, as He Himself declares: 'I and the Father are one' (Jn 10:30). Finally, on account of their very inseparability it suffices at times to name the Father alone, or the Son alone, as the one whose countenance will fill us with joy.[176]

HEART IN RELATION TO OTHER FACULTIES

The Eye of the Heart

The contemplation of the Trinity requires the faculty of sight, for Augustine asks: What else is pure contemplation, but to behold the Divine countenance and to rest in His luminescence? Accurate vision requires perfect health, especially of heart, for the other faculties draw strength from an impeccable heart. From whom does the heart seek health? None other than the Divine Physician: Nothing this-worldly has the power to restore the faculties for their heavenly purpose.[177] Sadly, since sin entered the world through Adam, we so easily develop the habit of seeking a cure from charlatans who appear to us in the guises of immoral behavior and false teachings.

Augustine laments the many years he stubbornly refused to believe this truth. He was a full grown man of not inconsequential fame. He whom others had admired for the vivacity of his rhetorical skills, found himself being consumed by his own vanity. Yet, he continued to seek vivification in the satisfaction of the flesh and

in vain intellectual pursuits as an auditor of the Manichean ide-
al. As he neared giving his full assent to Manichaeism, his sharp
intellect perceived the hollowness of its arguments and the con-
trasting soundness of Catholic teaching, especially as expounded
by Ambrose. Augustine praises God for being merciful to him.
Instead of abandoning Augustine as he became increasingly more
discontented, God drew closer to him, awakening inner discernment of his false beliefs and wretched moral condition.[178]

In the grip of his former teachers, Augustine believed that
only matter *mattered*. He confesses he was "unable to think any
substance possible other than that which the eyes normally perceive."[179] Later, through eyes illumined by faith, he reflects on the
dreadful condition of those who continue to engage in vain pursuits: "Now the goods I sought were no longer in the external
realm, nor did I seek for them with bodily eyes in the light of
the sun. In desiring to find their delight in externals, they easily
become empty and expend their energies on 'the things which
are seen and temporal' (2 Cor 4:18)."[180] Seeking goods — the
Good — in God's works but without Him, blackens the heart
and blinds the eye. Seeking the good in God's saving deeds and in
His imprint on His works, cleanses the heart and opens the eyes
to behold His countenance in the countenances of His children.
For, Augustine says, "We are not 'the light that illuminates every
man' (Jn 1:9). We derive our light from You, so that we 'who were
once darkness are light in You' (Eph 5:8)."[181]

The light of the Trinity is supernatural; hence, what is base
cannot perceive it. Since God's nature is pure spirit, we need more
than bodily eyes to see Him. The Beatific Vision is reserved for,
what Augustine terms, "the eye of the heart."[182] This faculty was
created by God for the purpose of gazing upon His countenance.
In the post-lapsarian life, the eye of the heart is closely aligned
with the will, and Augustine uses the terms synonymously at
times, for the eye is, essentially, our intentions. For instance, the
concupiscent eye intends morally corrupt thoughts and actions,

and the pure eye intends single-minded devotion to God. What the eye intends, it reaps: the former blindness and eternal death; the latter the vision of God and eternal life.[183]

Augustine states that the eye of the heart must undergo rigorous training to maintain the purity of its intentions. The eye gains strength and endurance by actively concentrating on God as we see Him and receive Him in the mysteries of the Christian faith. This endeavor must become a habit of the will, thus as we believe, the "mind's eye" is cleansed to see and receive Truth.[184] Augustine calls us to task:

> But first, 'wash, be clean, remove malice from your souls and from the sight of my eyes' that the dry land may appear. 'Learn to do good; judge in favor of the orphan and vindicate the widow' that the land may produce pasture and fruitful trees. 'And come, says the Lord, let us reason together' (Is 1:16-18), so that lights may be made in the firmament of heaven and give light over the earth. The rich man inquired of the good Master what he should do to obtain eternal life (Mt 19:16-22). ... Follow the Lord 'if you wish to be perfect.' Join the society of those among whom He 'speaks wisdom' (1 Cor 2:6), for He knows what belongs to the day and what to the night; then you too may know that.[185]

The tasks we accomplish are motivated by love, for how can Love, Himself, be sought, if love does not seek? Augustine tells us God has promised to shine His countenance upon us; in fact, His countenance has already been revealed through the Incarnation. How do we gaze upon Him? With the eyes of the body, we look at Him but do not see Him. With the eyes of the heart, we turn to Him and perceive His loveliness truly, but partially, however, ever more clearly as we conform our hearts to His. And what is this conformation, but Love? Augustine speaks of the heart's longing: "Let our heart speak thus to Him; 'I have sought Thy countenance; Thy face, O Lord, will I still seek. Turn not away Thy face from me' (Ps 26:8-10). And let Him reply to the plea of our hearts: 'He who loves me keeps my commandments; and he who loves me will be loved by my Father, and I will love him and manifest myself to him' (Jn 14:21)."[186]

HEART AND MIND

Of the Christian way of life, Augustine writes that we see God with the mind, rather than the eyes. Moreover, when the eyes seek rest from the sufferings of this world, they find they are helpless and are further agitated. In these two statements, Augustine seems to be contradicting himself, for elsewhere he teaches that we see God with the eye of the heart. The key to understanding the cogency of his arguments is to place both eye and mind in the center of the heart and to lift this trinity of faculties away from the temporal realm and into the spiritual realm, while simultaneously preserving the creaturely gifts of reason and sense, for the gifts of nature are imprinted with the supernatural. The mind as rational understanding arguably bears the strongest resemblance to the Divine Life.[187]

Augustine explains that at the instant the mind forms an image, we imbue what we imagine with our own essence. As relational beings, we cannot help but perceive what is external to us from our own point of reference. The rational mind passes judgment on the object of understanding and forms relationships of varying degrees of unity. Augustine's reference point is God, who favors those most resembling Him and, at the last, transfigures all who have acquired His mind through surrender of self to His will. The mind, then, is created in order to bind itself to the image of God above all and to forge unions with others for the love of Him. Augustine speaks of the eye of the mind, which means the faculty of introspection, that is, self-examination as nexus to truth. The eye of the mind perceives one's interior life as a relational being and uncovers God's love and handiwork.[188]

Unfortunately, the mind falters when it unites with its own images apart from God; it remains less than God intended. Rejecting its supernatural gift of grace, the mind becomes a caricature of itself. Its capacity to understand is stunted and cannot surpass the bodily level, replete with errors. The greatest misunderstanding is the confusion of true love with wanton desire. Experience trumps knowledge; privation corrupts the heart; the body kills the spirit. The mind has thus reaped what it has sown. Augustine counsels his hearers to understand a critical truth: "This turning away and turning toward result in the just punishment of unhappiness, because they are committed, not under compulsion, but voluntarily."[189]

The free choice the mind makes for evil causes our demise — not God, who alone is the author of our salvation, for even the freedom of the mind to choose for good or for ill is God's unmerited gift to us. His gift is enfleshed in the mind of the Son of Man who chose to die that we might live. God's mind is truth and life. Augustine counsels:

> [God speaks] by truth itself, if anyone is prepared to hear with the mind rather than with the body. For He speaks to that part of man which is better than all else that is in him, and than which God Himself alone is better. For since man is most properly understood (or, if that cannot be, then at least, *believed*) to be made in God's image, no doubt it is that part of him by which he rises above those lower parts he has in common with the beasts, which brings him nearer to the Supreme. But since the mind itself, though naturally capable of reason and intelligence, is disabled by besotting and inveterate vices not merely from delighting and abiding

in, but even from tolerating His unchangeable light, until it has been gradually healed, and renewed, and made capable of such felicity, it had, in the first place, to be impregnated with faith, and so purified. And that in this faith it might advance the more confidently towards the truth, the truth itself, God, God's Son, assuming humanity without destroying His divinity, established this faith, that there might be a way for man to man's God through a God-man.[190]

Memory is the most effective aid to the purified mind. Once the heart is struck by the love of God, the mind perceives the Trinity's supremacy over all and commits that knowledge to memory. The unfolding of the mysteries of faith stretched out in time are stored in the memory, drawn upon as nourishing milk in times of distress. Augustine calls memory the "stomach of the mind; whereas, gladness and sadness are like sweet and bitter food."[191] Through the power of recollection, we can feast on the good and remain hopeful despite the bad, for within memory is the imprint of the Trinity. While we experience memory as a temporal gift, it is eternal as it remembers and knows the love of God. The memory, understanding, and love of the Trinity, especially as we remember, understand and love Christ, enable the eye to see beyond the mortal into immortality, the heart to cleave to Him, and the will to stretch beyond the self to the Other. Augustine prays:

What then ought I to do, my God? You are my true life. I will transcend even this my power which is called memory. I will rise beyond it to move towards You, sweet light. What are You saying to me? Here I am climbing up through my mind towards You who are constant above me. I will pass beyond even that power of mind which is called memory, desiring to reach You by the way through which You can be reached, and to be bonded to You by the way in which it is possible to be bonded.[192]

Concomitant with memory is intuition and expectation. Time is calibrated by the mind into three movements: "the present of the past," which is remembrance; "the present of the present," intuition; and "the present of the future," expectation.[193] Without remembrance, however, expectation would succumb to despair. Remembrance raises knowledge to the level of wisdom through sight, and wisdom conveys hope, for wisdom "consists in the contemplation of eternal things." The eye of the heart is the faculty which glimpses dimly the Beatific Vision. The eye sees the mind's knowledge as truth, and it looks to the future for immutable happiness which, Augustine says, is in reality "joy grounded in truth."[194]

The heart is the receptacle of the partial happiness which the eye sees and the mind knows in the present life. The heart is filled with joy according to the measure of its chaste vision and wisdom. Without chastity, what is seen is an illusion, and what is known is a falsehood.[195] Contrariwise, Augustine assures us that God rewards the heart that loves with a pure mind, for "when the mind is carried up to God in this love, it will soar above all torture free and glorious, with wings beauteous and unhurt, on which chaste love rises to the embrace of God... and yet... we may see with what force the mind presses on with unflagging energy, in spite of all alarms, towards that it loves; and we learn that we should bear all things rather than forsake God, since those men bear so much in order to forsake Him."[196]

The chaste heart capable of bearing all things for God's embrace, requires a pure mind to concentrate the will on acquiring virtue. Love is the crown of the virtues and their reward, but forbearance is the means to love. We can develop the habits of temperance, fortitude, prudence, and justice, but if we do not forebear, all our efforts are for naught. Once we begin to live out the virtues in our mortal lives, they become implanted in our minds; thus the mind perceives the unity of virtue and the vision of God and beckons the will to incline towards forbearance. The perfection of these virtues requires supernatural grace; thus Augustine reminds us that perfection alone is capable of beholding the vision of God. By nature we can live well, but by grace we can live sanctified, for without grace, lust infiltrates the mind and distracts it from its striving to attain the wisdom of God. With grace, the mind is renewed according to God's likeness.[197] Augustine calls our attention to the words of Scripture on renewal of the mind:

> 'Stripping yourself of the old man with his deeds, put on the new man, that is beginning to be renewed in the knowledge of God, according to the image of Him who created him' (Col 3:9-10)… this renewal and reformation of the mind is made according to God or according to the image of God. [St. Paul] says 'according to God,' therefore, that we might not think it to be made according to another creature; but 'according to the image of God,' therefore, that we might understand this renewal to be wrought in that thing where there is the image of God, namely, in the *mind*.[198]

The renewed mind knows itself, and it loves itself truly. The presence of mind, knowledge, and love in the heart of the person forms a trinity, after God's image and likeness. Augustine sees the resemblance between the trinity of mind, knowledge, and love, and the Divine Trinity of Father, Son, and Spirit. He explains that "there is no confusion through any commingling, although each is a substance in itself, and all are found mutually in all…. These three, therefore, are in a marvelous manner inseparable from one another; and yet each of them is substance, and all together are one substance or essence, while the terms themselves express a mutual relationship."[199] The mind fully cognizant of itself, loves itself, and vice versa. Perfection does not thrive in isolation; thus perfection, that is purity, radiates through all the faculties until God's perfection is all in all.[200]

Heart and Will

The will is the faculty which moves the heart towards or away from the Beatific Vision. As the mover, its nature is freedom; its character is responsibility; its function is creativity; its purpose is goodness. God endowed humankind with a free will according to His own free will. With freedom comes the responsibility to accept God's grace by obeying His will. The upright will determines actions and, by extension, fashions the heart. The whole person becomes upright.[201]

While freedom of the will was discussed earlier in Chapter Two, it is worth reiterating a few brief pointed remarks about Augustine's understanding of the condition of the will before and after the Fall and within the Beatific Vision.

> The first freedom of the will was in being able not to sin; the final freedom will be much greater — in not being able to sin. The first immortality was in being able not to die; the final immortality will be much greater — in not being able to die. The first power of perseverance was in being able not to forsake good; the final power will be the blessedness of perseverance — in not being able to forsake good. Because these latter gifts are better and more desirable, the former gifts are not therefore of no account or of small account... the aids themselves are to be distinguished. One is an aid without which something is not done; the other, by which something is done.[202]

The free nature of the will has undergone a debilitating

transformation since Adam sinned. From humanity's beginning, the will has drawn its power from God by His grace. Since the first rejection of grace through original sin, the will's free nature is present, albeit crushingly weakened. Lacking the fullness of faith in God's omnipotence, the will runs willy-nilly after fleeting temptations of the flesh, thereby enervating its power and reducing its freedom. The limp will retains its freedom to choose, Augustine maintains, for "the will could not become evil, were it unwilling to become so."[203] The risk to freedom is that by choosing evil, the will may become irreparably deficient. The mutuality of faculties ensures that a deficient will leads to deficiency in sight, reason, and affections. Even in its deficient movements, however, the will and all the faculties of the human person are goods of creation, for without them, a righteous life is impossible. Always, according to God's persevering will, there is the possibility of conversion towards the Good; thus despair is precluded no matter how great a deficiency exists. Augustine accepts the mysterious relationship between freedom of the will and God's gift of perseverance, thus he admonishes us to act towards the hope of salvation for us and for our neighbor: "Since we cannot distinguish the predestined from those who are not predestined, and for this reason must will that all should be saved, we must administer to all the strong medicine of admonition, lest any should perish, or cause the ruin of others…. God will make our admonitions useful to 'those whom He has foreknown and predestined to become conformed to the image of His Son' (Rm 8:29)."[204]

Free will is characterized by responsibility; gift and task are inseparable. Original sin does not eradicate the gift, for the God who is constancy will not take back what He has done. Rather, by the free choice of our will, we have misused the gift, effecting a declination of the gift *as given* by the Creator. Because we refused the task through sin, which debilitated the will, it will be that much more difficult to resume the task and impossible without grace. The character of the will is determined by the degree of responsibility the will assumes. The will that moves the heart to cleave to eternal things will be rewarded with the Trinity's embrace, while the will that moves the heart towards the satisfaction of fleeting pleasures will incur God's wrath.[205]

The debilitated will requires sanctifying grace to act responsibly. The Giver does not fail, for He sanctifies the will through Baptism, that it may grow in freedom and responsibility. Grace restores the ability to persevere in willing, in spite of weakness. Without grace, there is no power to persevere; without the will, there is no will to persevere. According to God's design, grace and will are mutually related. The sanctified will, Augustine says, "is unwaveringly and invincibly influenced by divine grace" to move the heart nearer to God.[206]

The will functions creatively when it acts responsibly, for it fashions itself according to God's design. Augustine teaches: "All things owe to God, first of all, what they are insofar as they are natures. Then, those who have received a will owe to Him whatever better thing they can will to be, and whatever they ought to be.... [If] he has received free will and sufficient power, he stands under obligation."[207]

The Creator is immovable; however, creation is not. The Good is changeless, but goods possess fluidity. In fact, Augustine tells us the unchangeable Good makes possible the existence of changeable goods. An act of the will is necessary for change, and an act of the will assisted by grace is the prerequisite for positive change. For the soul to be good, the will must acquiesce to the Good; for the heart to be pure, the will must relinquish impurity; for the mind to know God, the will must accept the Wisdom of God; for the eye to behold God, the will must love God.[208]

God gave us free will that we might choose Him without compulsion. Although we are powerless against His might, He will not force us to love Him. Instead, He woos us through Christ's sacrificial acts of love. The will, so enamored with this lavish gift, wills one thing only, to be the Son's chaste bride for-

ever. Once the Bridegroom's proposal is accepted, the will must
cleave to Him who is the Supreme Good. In this manner, the will
becomes single-minded in purpose; thus in willing the Good, the
whole person becomes good. What, then, is good will? Augustine
answers: "It is that by which we seek to live rightly and honorably.... Whoever wants to live rightly and honorably, if his will
for this surpasses his will for temporal goods, achieves this greater
good so easily that to have what he wills is nothing other than the
act of willing."[209] The good will assisted by grace becomes strong
in virtue and unwavering in devotion. Pure in heart, the consummation of joy is at hand.[210]

Heart and Body

The final consummation occurs between Christ, the Bridegroom, and the whole person — body and soul. For Augustine,
the body and its capacity for conjugal love are goods. Peter Brown
in *The Body and Society* points out that Augustine's understanding
is a departure from the prevailing view of his predecessors who
taught that marriage, sexuality, and the family were post-lapsarian features of human relationships, i.e., consequences of original
sin.[211] Augustine argues that the sexual characteristics and functions of the body were the same before the Fall as after. Accordingly, this was a great good, intended by God as the fulfillment of
human friendship and the command to procreate as families.[212]

Augustine opines that, congruent with God's design, the
body would be subject to the will which, in turn, would perfectly
submit to God. With the Fall, however, the will refused to submit,
and chaos ensued. The body, now subject to a renegade will, suffers under the will's inclination — and acquiescence — to mul-
titudinous temptations. Some sufferings are alleviated when the
will chooses to return to God; however, others remain, like physical corruption and death of the body. Augustine notes the obvious
effect of original sin on the body: "For no sooner do we begin to

live in this dying body, than we begin to move ceaselessly towards death. For in the whole course of this life (if we must call it) its mutability tends towards death... so that our whole life is nothing but a race towards death... all are driven forwards with an impartial movement, and with equal rapidity."[213]

Death is not the consequence of the body's transgressions, but that of the will, for the body lacks the power to sin. Even the mind, which is part of the body, does not cause sin, as there is no hierarchy of strengths among minds, although a wise mind may desire to avoid sin. The will, alone, has the strength to cause sin, effecting corruption and the disruption of the right ordering of the goods of creation. When the will lives for itself, it debases both the body and soul — the *heart* of the person. The decrepit physical manifestations of sin on the body signify the heart's interior foulness. Only the regenerative effects of grace can cleanse the heart trapped within a decaying body and, at the resurrection of the dead, restore the body to perfection, as well.[214]

The Trinity's image within the body is damaged, but not erased, as a result of original sin. Augustine points to the evidence of this great blessing in the countless ways God reveals Himself in physical bodies of every sort, but especially in the trinities associated with the human body: "The trinity of the outer man appeared first of all, in those things that are perceived without, that is, from the body that is seen, from the form imprinted hereby in the gaze of the beholder, and from the attention of the will which combines both."[215]

Indeed, we can see beautiful handiwork in physical being; however, Augustine warns us not to make false gods out of what our eyes behold. Instead, look beyond this lower beauty to the highest, from whom all loveliness is derived. The faculty with which we see is the eye of the heart, purified under the impulse of the will that is grounded in faith in Jesus Christ. Augustine proclaims:

'*Blessed are the pure in heart, for they shall see God.*' For the eyes needed in order to see this good are not those with which we see the light spread through space, which has part in one place and part in another, instead of being all in every place. The sight and the discernment we are to purify is that by which we see, as far as is allowed in this life, what is just, what is pious, what is the beauty of wisdom. He who sees these things, values them far above the fullness of all regions in space, and finds that the vision of these things requires not the extension of his perception through distances in space, but its invigoration by an immaterial influence.[216]

Heart and Soul

Purity of heart and the vision of God are not achieved without struggle, for the corruptible body presses down upon the soul, which through the will experiences the oppressive burden of human nature. The soul, however, cannot blame corrupted flesh for its own depravity; rather, the soul, corrupted by sin, lays waste the flesh. The body is an essential good, necessary for the soul's fulfillment of beatitude.[217] The soul is the principal good of the body, that is, the "heart" of the person. The soul is either depraved or chaste, depending on the movement of the will towards or away from the Supreme Good. The soul that adheres to God is the good soul, as God, Himself, is *the* Good. Contrariwise, if the soul seeks the sinful pleasures "by vanity and baneful curiosity," then the world, with the Devil at its helm, becomes lord of the soul.[218] Humanity's fleshly nature does not cause a soul to become like the Devil, as the fallen angels are not made of flesh. Instead, it is by sharing the Devil's lust to live for himself that effects the soul's demise. Augustine reiterates St. Paul's directive to the Romans: "'Be not conformed to this world' (Rm 12:2) — for the point is to show that a man is conformed to whatever he loves — to this authority."[219] If the soul's authority is the decay of sinful flesh, it follows that the soul will rot, as well. The mortal body suffers death in time as a consequence of original sin. The corrupt immortal soul suffers both the death of the body and an eternal death, as a consequence of its abandonment of God.[220]

To escape the punishment of everlasting death, the soul's task in life must be to use and enjoy the goods of this world for God's sake, according to the intention for which they were made. In this manner, concupiscence is absent from the relationship between God's will and the use and enjoyment of the world's bounty. The soul cannot accomplish this task on its own apart from God, as through original sin, concupiscence acts like an infectious disease upon the soul from birth.

To carry out its charge, the soul undergoes a second birth through Baptism, receiving the Holy Spirit's sanctifying grace. The presence of sanctifying grace sharpens the faculties of the heart: the eye to see divine beauty in creation; the ear to hearken to God's voice above the world's cacophonies; the mind to understand the doctrines of the faith; the will to cleave to these. Then the soul, as part of God's holy Church, becomes faithful and through righteous acts of an upright will, lives accordingly.[221] This is the soul living out its purpose. Augustine teaches that God sends souls for two reasons. One is to enliven the body, for the soul is the body's chief good, and the other is to overcome the punishment of sin by preparing for the Beatific Vision — the "place of heavenly incorruption."[222] Augustine instructs us that "it does so by being well controlled, that is by being purified by virtue and submitting to the rightful servitude ordained of God's creation."[223] The soul must, therefore, be ontologically pure in order to possess the capacity to see God.

Augustine regards the soul as a citizen soldier engaged in a battle between two rival cities: the city of God and the city of this world. The war's outcome is secured by the promises of Christ; the victory is won. A soul, though, may persist in bearing arms

for the losing side. The soldier who chooses the weapons of carnal lust will die with the collapse of the city; however, the soldier
who dons the armor of faith will share in the victory.[224] Augustine
lauds the wise soul who possesses the endurance and courage to
stay the course, because the eye of the heart is focused on the final
glory, the mind plots the course, and the will is inclined towards
this happy end.

> When we are eager to be wise, we simply, and as quick-
> ly as we can, find some means of concentrating our
> whole soul on the object; when it is attained by the
> mind, we fix it there firmly, not so that the soul may
> rejoice in its own private pleasure — which involves
> only fleeting pleasures — but so that the soul, free of
> all inclination toward things of time and space, may
> grasp that which is one, the same, and eternal. *As the
> soul is the whole life of the body, so God is the happy life
> of the soul.* This is the undertaking in which we are
> engaged, and toward which we will strive until we have
> completed it. It has been granted to us to enjoy these
> true and certain goods which gleam before us, however
> obscured they may have been until this stage of our
> journey. Is this not what was written of wisdom's treat-
> ment of its lovers, when they approach and seek it? It
> is said, 'In the ways it will show itself to them joyfully
> and in all providence it will meet them.' Wherever you
> turn, wisdom speaks to you through the imprint it has
> stamped upon its works.[225]

"As the soul is the whole life of the body, so God is the happy
life of the soul."[226] There is no middle road for the soul; rather,
set before the soul is an either/or proposition. The soul, born of
an unchaste union, may not live unchastely towards the vision of
God: The soul's ignoble birth is not an excuse for a debauched

life. The imprint of God's Wisdom on the soul inculcates a restless spirit on the heart and a gnawing presence in the mind. Heart and mind, then, intuitively know the incompleteness of this life and groan towards the fulfillment of a happy rest. The soul which chooses to wallow in the circumstances of its unholy birth will groan in unremitting agony; however, the soul sanctified through Baptism and growing in holiness through chastity will groan in *hopeful* travail towards the fulfillment of joy. By the sinful flesh both were born of Adam; by the chaste flesh of the Son of God, both receive the promise of justification. By rejecting the chastity of the Son, one soul will be lost; by accepting the Son through a pure heart, the other soul will be found in the happy life.[227]

5

Purity as a State of Being

One's arrival at the Beatific Vision — the heavenly state of perfect happiness where one knows, loves, and serves God in His fullness — requires a transformation of the heart. The heart must be so disposed that it sees God alone. Gertrude Gillette, writing about purity of heart in early ascetic literature, discusses some of the many ways Augustine expresses this teaching in words: "'purity of heart,' 'simplicity of heart,' a 'clean heart,' and a 'single' or 'simple heart.'"[228] When Augustine speaks of heart, he is not using the term in an abstract way, but in an intensely personal manner. One must look at one's own interior disposition. God gives the promise. Will I attain it? It is "my" soul which matters. The communion of saints is composed of individual souls united by a harmony of purity, unique to each yet common to all.[229]

The acquisition of this pure state requires both the movement of God through grace and the soul's free choice of the will. God first cleansed us through the Incarnation of the Son. Here He gave us a "beginning" in the eternal life, and He set us on the right path through the gift of faith. The human will undergoes daily cleansing by adhering to faith in the Son and practicing the virtues unfeigned. This is the road to perfection; whereby, in the distention of time, the soul has "followed Him in some measure to that place to which He has ascended."[230] With each step along the road, the soul sheds the baseness of its birth in concupiscence and acquires the loftiness of God: The soul comes to resemble the One whom it strives to reach. The soul sees God according to the measure in which the soul resembles God, thus the happy state in the life to come is lived in the present life incompletely, yet truly.[231]

DETACHED LOVE

Following God is the sole means to happiness. Sadly, due to original sin, we are precluded from seeing Him clearly, and the actual sins we commit in life further obscure that path. God, however, is merciful towards us. Out of compassion for the plight of our inadequate senses, He has lit a lamp, so to speak. Augustine directs us to the luminescence of holy writ: Hold steadfast to Scripture, for the truths contained within are the wisdom of God, who gives us the capacity to understand according to the firmness of our faith. Those who are single-minded in faith may vary widely in worldly knowledge; however, they are equally wise in the Lord. Scripture reveals the living Word of God and draws us into His loving embrace. We cleave to the Son by love — the same love which He poured out to us in His incarnation, life, passion, death, and resurrection.[232]

Love is the desire of the heart for the beloved. Holy love is a share in the charity of God which moves the mind to know God and the eye of the heart to see God. Augustine instructs us "to remain in this [good] and cling to it by love, that we may enjoy the presence of that from which we are, in the absence of which we would not be at all. For since 'we walk by faith, not by sight' (2 Cor 5:7), we certainly do not yet see God, as [St. Paul] has said: 'face to face' (1 Cor 13:12). Unless we love Him now, we shall never see Him."[233]

Love's Weight Bears All

Augustine argues that we experience inertia as a result of the crushing weight of sin bearing down on our souls. A greater weight is needed to remove this millstone and bear aloft the soul towards its heavenly goal. The weight which moves the soul towards everlasting joy is love — the love of God in the love of the human person. The fulfillment of God's promise to redeem humanity is found in the dead weight of His Son — His *Beloved* — hanging on a cross. The fulfillment of God's promise of personal salvation is found in the weight of His love in a person's heart. Augustine writes: "Love lifts us there, and 'Your good Spirit' (Ps 142:10) exalts 'our humble estate from the gates of death' (Ps 9:15). In a good will is our peace."[234]

The paradox of Divine Love's weight is in its *weightlessness*; that is, the heart weighted by God's love is released from the weight of the world. The faith-filled will, inclined towards the Good, moves the heart to unburden itself from the divided loves of this world, and it stretches upward in single-minded devotion to the one undivided love of the Trinity. Augustine depicts the will's ascent by drawing on the language of the psalms:

> My weight is my love. Wherever I am carried, my love is carrying me. By Your gift we are set on fire and carried upwards: We grow red hot and ascend. We climb 'the ascents in our heart' (Ps 83:6) and sing 'the song of steps' (Ps 119:1). Lit by Your fire, Your good fire, we grow red-hot and ascend, as we move upwards 'to the peace of Jerusalem' (Ps 121:6), 'For I was glad when they said to me, let us go to the house of the Lord' (Ps 121:1). There we will be brought to our place by a good will, so that we want nothing but to stay there forever.[235]

Augustine confesses the poignancy of the heart's acquiescence to the weight of Divine Love. Amidst the joy of true love
gained, the heart feels the bittersweet pangs of remembrance of
loves lost by its own accord through concupiscence. The memory
of past divided loves acts as a watchman over the renewed heart,
fortifying the will to stay the course. Divine Providence favors
the regenerated heart with an intensity of happiness and a fervent
longing to rest eternally and perfectly happy.[236]

The love-filled heart is made ready to combat the temptations of the flesh, as well as the trials of suffering in this world.
Here the weight of love acts as an impenetrable army against the
forces of evil, and for Augustine, his own most crushing weight
of sin was his sexual incontinence. Love is constant; concupiscence — in whatever way it manifests itself — is ever changing.
The corruptible flesh quickly grows weary of fleeting pleasures
and becomes increasingly debilitated each time it seeks satisfaction in evil. On the other hand, Divine Charity is indefatigable;
therefore, *sanctified* love grows stronger as the heart patiently and
determinedly detaches from earthly delights. In this way, temptation purifies the heart.[237]

Tribulation — suffering — is a more intense refining fire to
cleanse the heart, even than temptation. Suffering is both purgative and creative. Echoing the words of St. Paul to the Romans,
Augustine calls us to rejoice over our sufferings, as they build endurance to finish the race. When we follow the Savior, primarily
in the way He suffered, we take on His virtues, especially the
virtue of the *certain* hope of the heavenly prize. Indeed, our tribulations are a prize because they are a share in the Son of Man's
tribulations on earth, chiefly His passion. Here in His suffering
love, the Holy Spirit perfectly discharges God's own charity into
our hearts.[238]

ASSAULTS ON LOVE

Augustine's yoking of God's charity with Christ's suffering love defines the form of human love. Charity, the supernatural gift of self-emptying for the sake of another, requires sacrifice. God, through Christ, emptied Himself for us on the cross in an act of unsurpassable suffering. We who are born into sin must empty ourselves of all its evil consequences by our single-minded devotion to God and imitation of His self-emptying love, through our personal travails and mortal death.[239]

Unfortunately, because of sin we are inclined to confuse true charity with desire — the passion of Christ with the disordered passions of the flesh, that is, concupiscence. Augustine determines this happens when our passions are devoid of reason, moved solely by *feelings*. Love — informed by the light of reason and guided by faith — works for good, independent of feelings, which are chameleons under the sway of the desires of the flesh. Love draws us to moral heights; feelings drag us into moral decrepitude.[240]

Augustine perceives a battle raging within each person between charity and concupiscence. Because we are unconditionally loved by God, we *love* love, itself, and desire the happy life only love can bestow. Because our hearts are deformed by sin, we also are repulsed by love. Rather, we lust after trifles, thereby hating the good we ought to love. Love and hate, then, coexist in an oppositional relationship within the same person until one emerges the victor.[241]

Augustine draws upon his own experiences to illustrate the violence of this war. It is precisely because the light of truth is not extinguished in us and in the beauty of creation that we long for truth's fulfillment; however, because of concupiscence, we find ourselves drawn back into the habit of sin. Indeed, the fleeting delights of the flesh are easily satisfied, while we must wait patiently for the permanence of the Beatific Vision.

Sometimes You cause me to enter into an extraordinary depth of feeling marked by a strange sweetness. If it were brought to perfection in me, it would be an experience quite beyond anything in this life. But I fall back into my usual ways under my miserable burdens. I am reabsorbed by my habitual practices. I am held in their grip. I weep profusely, but still I am held. Such is the strength of the burden of habit. I am in misery.[242]

Surely, Augustine opines, we all strive for the happy life which is nothing more than "joy grounded in truth."[243] However, there are those who make themselves enemies of truth, in spite of their happy goal. Augustine counted himself among that sorry lot before he came to the Catholic faith. With great precision, he describes their perverse love: "Their love for truth takes the form that they love something else and want this object of their love to be the truth; and because they do not wish to be deceived, they do not wish to be persuaded that they are mistaken. And so they hate the truth for the object which they love instead of the truth. They love truth for the light it sheds, but hate it when it shows them up as being wrong (Jn 3:21; 5:35)."[244]

They turn inward to their own spirit rather than face their error, admit their culpability, and turn to God. Augustine describes the rational spirit as being "different from God and yet second only to God."[245] Indeed, the spirit occupies the loftiest space among all God's creations and, Augustine holds, becomes "even nobler when it forgets itself in its love of the immutable God; or when, in the depths of its being, it despises itself by comparison with Him."[246] The spirit relinquishes its elevated perch, however, when it becomes self-satisfied and ignores God, whose lofty abode is unreachably higher. Augustine laments the consequences of such a spirit, "seeking to imitate God in a perverse way, so that it wills to delight in its own power… the more it desires to be greater, the less it becomes."[247]

This is pride: the self-satisfaction we feel for our own deeds; the merit we claim for our goodness; the joy we experience in our power; our lust for the accolades of others. Augustine cringes at such vanity, for he has personally come to know the misery of that corrupt life. He confesses: "This is the main cause why I fail to love and fear You in purity. Therefore 'You resist the proud but give grace to the humble' (1 P 5:5). You 'thunder upon the ambitions of the world,' and 'the foundations of the hills tremble' (Ps 17:4, 8)."[248]

The proud strive to reach God through a perverse imitation of Him. Instead of finding happiness in God's providence, they sink to despair, as they see in others the same deceit and wickedness that exists in them. Still, the sinful habit prevails, and the proud who cannot find a loving communion with God and those who love Him in the Church, settle for the moldering bonds of concupiscence existing among the proud in this world, that disintegrate into eternal death in the next.

> It becomes our pleasure to be loved and feared not for Your sake, but instead of You. By this method the Enemy makes people resemble himself, united with him, not in loving concord but in sharing a common punishment. The enemy is he who 'decided to place his throne in the north' (Is 14:13f.) so that in the dark and the cold, men should serve him who, by a perverted and twisted life, imitates You.[249]

Augustine counsels sinners never to lose hope, for the light of truth is not extinguished by sin; God's love is constant, whether or not one accepts it. Even those who have sunk to the depths of depravity continue to strive to reach God, albeit in twisted ways: they seek to acquire His attributes without Him. Augustine directs such sinners to search for the flicker of truth burning in the embers of their hearts, which yet sheds a faint glow in the ever darkening heart. He expresses his heart's desire in prayer, recollecting a time when he was on the brink of the abyss:

> May the truth of the light of my heart, not my darkness, speak to me. I slipped down into the dark and was plunged into obscurity. Yet from there, even from there I loved You. 'I erred and I remembered You' (Ps 118:176).... May I not be my own life. On my own resources I lived evilly. To myself I was death. In You I am recovering life.[250]

Augustine is confident God will favor the heart's slightest bending towards Him in contrition and supplication. His act of self-emptying for us on the cross has opened the way through which we can pass from death to life. This is "not a way that lies through space, but through a change of affections."[251] Squelch the desires of the flesh; relinquish the will to Him; open the eye of the heart to see Him; love Him with single-minded devotion. Augustine cries out:

> My God, give me Yourself, restore Yourself to me. See, I love You, and if it is too little, let me love You more strongly. I can conceive no measure by which to know how far my love falls short of that which is enough to make my life run to Your embraces, and not to turn away until it lies hidden 'in the secret place of Your presence' (Ps 30:21). This alone I know: without You it is evil for me, not only in external things but within my being, and all my abundance which is other than my God, is mere indigence.[252]

Friendship with God

The first "pang of penitence," Augustine confesses, drove him to his knees.[253] Such is the power of penitence, that at its impulse, one can offer one's life to God as an act of hope in His providence. Over many years Augustine lived self-satisfied, seeking the goods of this world, especially knowledge and fame, to suit his own desires. His will was the problem, and looking back, he sees the futility of his endeavors. His will had been inclined towards the goods of this world. He asks:

> And what is the object of my love? I asked the earth and it said: 'it is not I....' I asked the sea, the deeps, the living creatures... 'We are not your God; look beyond us....' I asked the breezes... heaven, sun, moon and stars.... I said to all these things in my external environment: 'Tell me of my God who you are not, tell me something about Him.' And with a great voice they cried out: 'He has made us' (Ps 99:3). My question was the attention I gave to them, and their response was their beauty.... Human beings can put a question so that 'the invisible things of God are understood and seen through the things which are made' (Rm 1:20). Yet by love of created things they are subdued by them, and being thus made subject become incapable of exercising judgment.... *But your God is for you the life of your life.*[254]

In his penitence — his illuminating moment — he recovered his free will in order to relinquish it to God. He discovered the paradox of the will; whereby, in renouncing his own will, he gained true freedom of the will. In offering himself to God as His *slave*, Augustine did not assume a heavier burden; rather, *God* took on Augustine's every burden. "'Thereby I submitted my neck to your easy yoke and my shoulders to your light burden' (Mt 11:30), O Christ Jesus 'my helper and redeemer' (Ps 18:15)."[255]

Augustine began his renewal in faith by rejecting his will and cleaving to God's will. What else is faith, but trust in the surety of God's friendship with the human race, particularly His superlative intimacy with the individual person. There could be no more intimate union for a person than "God and I." Augustine rejoices with God at that redemptive moment: "There You began to be my delight, and You gave 'gladness in my heart' (Ps 4:7)."[256] His gladness was so profound that nothing of this world he previously associated with delight could compare, even in the slightest way. The supernatural had pierced nature, and all his gaze was fixed on heaven: "I had no desire for earthly goods to be multiplied, nor to devour time and to be devoured by it. For in the simplicity of eternity I had another kind of 'corn and wine and oil' (Ps 4:9)."[257] At that "first pang of penitence" Augustine became acutely aware that all his former pursuits and delights — once so dear to his heart — had only served to consume his heart with rubbish. God used Augustine's contrition as a purifying astringent, preparing the heart to be filled by Him. Augustine recollects the instant when "suddenly it had become sweet to me to be without the sweets of folly. What I once feared to lose was now a delight to dismiss. You turned them out and entered to take their place."[258] God, Augustine proclaims, is his sufficiency.[259]

Augustine believes all suffer because of mortal nature. The greatest accolades, the most virtuous acts, the unsurpassed feats of the mind, pass like night into day, and aspirations fade. Despair engulfs the hearts of those who place their hope in these. There is only one way to escape dejection: faith in Christ, *the Way, the Truth,* and *the Life.* His incarnate life, His word of truth, and His way of the cross, provide irrevocable evidence of God's charity, His bond of friendship with His own. We see that He who is eternal assumed mortal flesh without any corruption of His being, thereby imparting to us a share in His immortal life. We respond through faith, yet even our faith is His gift of charity to us. Augustine states that "in order that faith may work through charity (see Gal 5:6), 'the charity of God is poured forth in our hearts by the Holy Spirit who has been given to us' (Rm 5:5)."[260]

God's charity is our life, that is, the Trinity in us. Indeed, Augustine proclaims, love is a trinity: "the lover, the beloved, and the love. What else is love, therefore, except a kind of life which binds or seeks to bind some two together, namely, the lover and the beloved?"[261] This trinity of love is present in carnal loves, too, but these avail nothing towards the cleansing of the heart for God's love. God's charity is meant for the heart which aspires to the heights of love. While the heart may not attain the highest abode here on earth, it knows where to find its true home and the course on which it must travel.[262]

Knowledge of God is integral to love of God. The mind which seizes upon God with a pure heart *knows* Him. God, once He has begun to be known, stirs the mind to inquire more. The eye of the heart perceives Him as the goal of being and thus believes. Knowing and believing, then, are integral to love. In earthly life they exist in a complementary relationship, sustaining love in the face of the inadequacies of knowledge and belief. When our knowledge of God is frustrated, love for Him prevails through our belief that He is God. When doubt threatens to sever our friendship with God, love is fortified because we know Him — and not ourselves — to be God.[263]

Only the heart cleansed by faith can know God, believe Truth, love the Good, and conform to Christ in the certain hope of everlasting happiness. This is the work of the Holy Spirit, who spreads the love of God among us.[264] Augustine speaks of the centrality of faith:

> Even before we are capable of seeing and perceiving God, as He can be perceived, which is granted to the clean of heart, for *'blessed are the clean of heart, for they shall see God,'* He must be loved by faith; otherwise, the heart cannot be cleansed so as to be fit and ready to see Him. For where are those three, faith, hope, and charity (see 1 Cor 13:13), for the building up of which

in the soul, all the divine books have been composed and work together, except in the soul that believes what it does not yet see, and hopes for and loves what it believes? Therefore, even He who is not known, but in whom one believes, is already loved.[265]

God is not known in His fullness, but He is known through His works and most intimately through His Son. Jesus Christ, our mediator between the Father and His creation, is sufficiently known, that we may receive His Holy Spirit's sanctifying action in our hearts. When we incorporate our hearts into His, our hearts change into pure receptacles of His grace, able one day to bear the Beatific Vision. The heart that is a friend of Jesus forever shares in the divine charity of the Trinity.[266]

Fraternal Charity

Baptism inaugurates the Holy Spirit's regenerative action in the soul which heretofore had been separated from the love of God, but now it is reconciled to God by putting on Christ. This is an act of friendship with the Trinity by conforming to the Second Person. Baptismal grace is sufficient for the regeneration of the soul from sin to grace — from sickness to health. Through God's gift to us of the free choice of the will, we can choose to continue in health or return to sickness unto death.[267]

Christ's love, filling our hearts, demonstrates the way to perfect health, which is the imitation of the depth of His love. The Son of God who is unfathomably higher than we, became human so as to show us how the perfection of humanity loves. The way of perfection is the way of self-emptying love, to give every ounce of oneself for the sake of another: as God gave His only Son to us; as the Son of God condescended to become man; as the Son of Man sacrificed Himself in the greatest act of extreme humility in His crucifixion.[268]

As God loved us, so we must love others. Augustine tells us "the perfection of love is set before us by the imitation of God the Father Himself" who commands us to love our enemies, be kind to those who despise us, and pray for our persecutors.[269] By acquiring these virtues, we fulfill God's intention for us from the beginning of human life: to share in the indivisible bonds of charity within the Trinity by loving one another with pure hearts. Augustine professes the divine intention for mutual love among persons: "Truly, we can think of no surer step towards the love of God than the love of man to man."[270]

The love of God seizes us in an instant; however, to attain perfect love we must patiently endure the test of fraternal love throughout life. Augustine tells us that it is impossible to love God with a pure heart if we are impure toward neighbors in our thoughts or actions. The corrupt heart loves the neighbor for its own sake; the pure heart loves the neighbor for God's sake. When we are charitable towards others for the benefit of their redemption, we gain our own salvation, for God rewards a merciful heart in kind. Augustine writes: "'Thou shalt love thy neighbor as thyself' (Mt 22:39). Now you love yourself suitably when you love God better than yourself. What, then, you aim at in yourself you must aim at in your neighbor, namely that he may love God with a perfect affection."[271]

We reach the highest Good by caring for the lower goods, especially the human person who is the loftiest good of God's creation. "Our love of neighbor," Augustine testifies, "is a sort of cradle of our love to God."[272] He echoes the words of St. Paul to support this truth: "Love does no wrong to a neighbor; therefore love is the fulfilling of the law." "We know that in everything God works for good with those who love Him, who are called according to His purpose" (Rm 13:10; 8:28, *RSV*).[273]

Our neighbor is not only the Father's gift of love to us, but His instruction in how to love. We do not see God with our plain sight, but we see our neighbor plainly. Because we are spirit as well as body, we have been given the capacity to love our neighbor *spiritually*, also. As our love towards neighbor ascends to loftier heights, so the eye of the heart is sharpened to see the Highest Love. When we love another for God's sake, we love God and behold Him with the inner sight of love. Augustine professes his confidence in the efficacy of fraternal charity:

> [See] how highly the Apostle John commends brotherly love: 'He who loves his brother,' he says, 'abides in the light, and there is no scandal in him' (1 Jn 2:10). It is evident that he has put the perfection of justice in brotherly love, for he in whom there is no scandal is surely perfect, and yet it seems that he has kept silent about the love of God. He would never have done so if he did not intend that God should be understood in brotherly love itself. For a little later on in the same epistle he expresses this most plainly in the following words: 'Beloved, let us love one another, because love is from God. And everyone who loves is born of God and knows God.'[274]

The longing for the Beatific Vision impels us to strive to love God wholly in body, mind, and soul. Our loving endeavors for the sake of God build up our brothers and sisters, as the whole Law and the Prophets depend on the two great commandments: love of God and love of neighbor as oneself (see Mt 22:37-40). Augustine explains the fulfillment of the law occurs through obedience to these commandments and the attainment of its prophecies. Augustine preaches: "Do you wish to love your God? You possess Him in Christ: 'In the beginning was the Word, and the Word was with God; and the Word was God.' Do you wish to love your neighbor? You possess him in Christ: 'The Word was made flesh and dwelt among us' (Jn 1:1, 14)."[275]

The heart which yearns to see God obeys these pivotal precepts with ardent faith. Augustine prays: "May His grace cleanse us; may He purify us by His assistance and His consolations."[276] Through purity of love, then, the soul takes flight beyond the confines of this world into the freedom of its heavenly abode. Augustine expresses the relationship between purity and longing for beatific sight: "It is that sight, therefore, which enraptures every rational soul with the desire of it, and the more ardent it is the purer it is, and the purer it is the more it rises to spiritual things, and the more it rises to spiritual things the more it dies to material things."[277]

THE UPRIGHT WILL

Power of the Will

The force behind the soul's ardent desire for the Beatific Vision is the good will, for the will drives our thoughts, words, and actions. The will, however, may work against desire when a bad will leads the soul, seeking happiness, off course. The will's power is great. It can lead the heart to be filled by God, the greatest good, or it can direct the heart to satiate its impassioned desires with trifles that leave the heart wanting.[278]

The crux of the matter lies in the inclination of the will towards the good. The good will, inclined towards God, seeks to satisfy the heart's longing for happiness by concentrating thoughts and accomplishing deeds that benefit the spiritual life. Contrariwise, the bad will inclined towards self-satisfaction, seeks to satiate the heart's longing for happiness by directing the mind and actions towards the building up of material successes. As life draws to a close, and the bad will has seen the unraveling of life's material gains, it will suffer unending agony at the realization that the happiness the soul desired has been eluded. The upright will, however, which strove for the unfailing good, will not be disappointed by life's travails and losses of material goods; rather, this soul will reap the reward of eternal bliss.[279]

Augustine poses the rhetorical question: "What lies more truly in the power of the will than the will itself?"[280] Here he explains that within the will is contained the power to delight in the good or to be found wanting. So great a gift is the will that, through free choice, the will possesses the potential to become regenerated through repentance and remission of sin. Augustine writes:

> While a man thinks that he is very unhappy if he has lost his fine reputation, great wealth, or various goods of the body, would you not consider him extremely unhappy even if he had an abundance of such things? For he is clinging to things that he can very easily lose and that he does not have while he wants them; he lacks moreover, the good will which is not to be compared to these and which, though it is so great a good, he needs only to will in order to possess.[281]

The will does not enter this world in pristine condition, inclined towards the good in all instances. The sad circumstances of the soul's birth into original sin produces a flabby will; thus the soul's solitary hope for an upright will is God's sanctifying grace, first and necessarily bestowed at Baptism, thereafter received sacramentally. The inclination towards sin remains in the will even after Baptism; however, the will which struggles to direct the heart towards *spiritual* fulfillment, progresses on the road to perfection. Augustine explains it is as if there are two wills engaged in battle within the person: the one tempted to be dragged down by the force of habitual concupiscence and the other overcoming itself to acquiesce to God's will. Augustine confesses:

> In my own case, as I deliberated about serving my Lord God (Jr 30:9) which I had long been disposed to do,

the self which willed to serve was identical with the self which was unwilling. It was I. I was neither wholly willing nor wholly unwilling. So I was in conflict with myself and dissociated from myself. The dissociation came about against my will. Yet this was not a manifestation of the nature of an alien mind but the punishment suffered in my own mind. And so it was 'not I' that brought this about 'but sin which dwelt in me' (Rm 7:17, 20), sin resulting from the punishment of a more freely chosen sin, because I was a son of Adam.[282]

Virtue and the Will

Augustine argues the "double" will is overcome by virtue, specifically the divine virtue of charity, which frees the will from the shackles of contradictory willing. The will discovers true freedom through the love of God in Christ, infused into the hearts of the faithful by the Holy Spirit as grace. Grace cleanses — *sanctifies* — the heart to receive the Redeemer's pure embrace of love and unfailing promise of the Beatific Vision.

'To those who are called we preach Christ the virtue of God, and the wisdom of God' (1 Cor 1:23f.).... [If] we ask what it is to live well, that is, to strive after happiness by living well, it must... be to love virtue, to love wisdom, to love truth, and to love with all the heart, with all the soul, and with all the mind; virtue which is inviolable and immutable, wisdom which never gives place to folly, truth which knows no change or variation from its uniform character.... 'No man comes to the Father but by me.' To this we cleave by sanctification. For when sanctified we burn with full and perfect love, which is the only security for our not turning away from God, and for our being conformed to Him rather than to this world; for 'He has predestinated us, that we should be conformed to the image of His Son' (Rm 8:29).[283]

Grace attracts the will to this truth, but grace does not constrain the will. When the will responds freely to truth by becoming a slave to the Divine Will, it becomes eternally free. Such is the inscrutable wisdom of Incarnate Love, that freedom is won through the free sacrifice of liberty: Christ freely sacrificed His freedom from sin to "become sin" in the Incarnation; we freely sacrifice our sinful will to gain a will free from sin.[284]

'Not everyone who has said to me, 'Lord, Lord,' shall enter into the kingdom of heaven but he who does the will of my Father who is in heaven, he shall enter into the kingdom of heaven' (Mt 5:21). We are not to think that if one merely addresses our Lord with 'Lord, Lord,' this has anything to do with those fruits, and we consequently put him down as a good tree. But the fruits consist in this — to do the will of the Father who is in heaven; and of how this is to be done He deigned to give Himself as an example.[285]

The free sacrifice of the will to Divine Charity occurs all at once in the rarest of cases, as in the miracle of Saul's conversion of heart on the road to Damascus. Instead, the slow and rocky path to the good will is the norm, as Augustine relates in his intimate *Confessions*. The way is charted through a cleansing of the corrupt heart by the training in virtue, beginning with humility, inseparable from charity — and groaning towards charity — the summit of all virtues. Augustine tells us our Lord chose to place humility as first in order of the beatitudes, after His own example of extreme humility. God in the Highest humbly submitted to the ignominy of a wretched birth in a stable, "for blessedness starts with humility: 'Blessed are the poor in spirit' (Mt 5:3), that is, those who are not puffed up, whose soul is submissive to divine authority, who stand in dread of punishment after this life despite the seeming blessedness of their earthly life."[286]

Because God is love, the attainment of the fullness of love is reserved for the heavenly estate, and only those hearts which have undergone the purgation of love through a steady growth in virtue, are capable of receiving love unalloyed.[287] Purgation involves suffering—intensely interior suffering. Although all suffer physically and emotionally as a consequence of evil in the world, these pains avail nothing for the cleansing of the heart if one does not suffer *all* for the sake of God. Augustine reminds his hearers to expect the world to heap agonies upon the Christian who is humble of heart, yet to accept persecution with gladness for the peace to come:

> 'Blessed are ye'... 'when they will revile you and perse-cute you and speak all that is evil against you, untruly, for my sake. Be glad and rejoice, for your reward is great in heaven' (Mt 5:11f.). Let him notice this — whoever seeks the delights of this world and the ad-vantage of temporal things ostensibly as a Christian — that our blessedness is within the soul; just as it is said with prophetic speech concerning the soul of a member of the Church: 'All the beauty of the king's daughter is within' (Ps 44:14). For from without are promised revilings and persecutions and calumnies; though for these the reward in heaven is great, which is experienced in the heart of those who endure them, who can already say: 'We glory in tribulation, knowing that tribulation works patience, and patience trial, and trial does not confound hope, because the charity of God is poured forth in our hearts by the Holy Spirit who is given to us' (Rm 5:3-5). It is not the enduring

of these things that brings reward, but bearing them for the name of Christ not only with unruffled soul but even with rejoicing.[288]

When we are tempted by discouragement from life's trials, we need only think of the humiliation of our Lord and that of His saints, who while they lived on earth were racked with suffering beyond comprehension; yet within their hearts they were glad. Their only suffering was the pain of not yet beholding God face to face; however, even this they endured for His sake because their hearts were so cleansed as to be little heavens on earth, humble dwelling places for our Savior to rest His Sacred Head.[289]

Virtue and blessedness exist in a reciprocal relationship. By the grace of God, each is the cause and fruit of the other. The saints were blessed because they lived an upright life; they were righteous because they were blessed. Through their prayers and by their lives, Augustine teaches, the saints exemplify the maxim that virtue is the way to see God.

> As to virtue leading us to a happy life, [it is] nothing else than perfect love of God. For the fourfold division of virtue [is taken] from four forms of love… temperance is love giving itself entirely to that which is loved; fortitude is love readily bearing all things for the sake of the loved object; justice is love serving only the loved object, and therefore ruling rightly; prudence is love distinguishing with sagacity between what hinders it and what helps it.[290]

The upright will live rightly, and a righteous life is a happy life. Augustine speaks of the congruence between happiness and righteousness: "Those who are happy, who also ought to be good, are not happy because they desire to live happily, which even evil men desire, but rather because they will to live rightly — which evil men do not."[291] The happy life then, is the reward for an upright will. "Merit," Augustine argues, "lies in the will."[292] He asks: "Is not justice the virtue according to which each man receives what is his due? ...Then whoever has good will [shall] embrace this one virtue with a devotion that considers that there is nothing better."[293]

While our hearts, stained by original sin, do not merit the Beatific Vision, God's love is more than just, and He wills the heart to know His justice through His mercy. Therefore, God, through grace, strengthens the assenting will to arouse the heart to cleave to Him. The heart engrafted to God becomes the virtue of God on earth and thus is transported to the perfection of virtue —justice, temperance, fortitude, prudence, courage, patience, charity — in heaven.

> Let a man will to be prudent, brave, temperate, just, and that he may be able to have these things truly, let him certainly desire power and seek to be powerful in himself, and strange as it may seem, to be against himself for himself. But as regards the rest of the things which he rightly wills and yet cannot obtain, such as immortality, and true and complete bliss, let him cease to desire them and patiently await them.[294]

Virtue bestows perfection on a graced soul; the soul becomes virtuous by following God; following God is the happy life; *the pure in heart shall see God.*[295]

The Single Heart

Single-Minded Virtue

> 'Blessed are the pure in heart, for they shall see God.'
> How foolish, therefore, are those who seek God with these outward eyes, since He is seen with the heart!

As it is written elsewhere, 'And in singleness of heart seek Him' (Wis 1:1). For that is a pure heart which is a single heart: and just as this light cannot be seen, except with pure eyes; so neither is God seen, unless that is pure by which He can be seen.[296]

Single-mindedness of heart and virtue are inseparable. The will that inclines to God through a virtuous life effects a transformation of the heart's devotion from self to God. Virtue acquired by the "single" heart is efficacious for the blessedness of oneself and towards the purity of heart of others, for virtue is not a solitary good. For instance, mercy is exercised upon another; temperance and fortitude influence moral choices; prudence regulates conduct; continence precludes exploitative gains; humility raises the dignity of self and neighbor. The communal dimension of virtue is not possible, however, unless virtue is acquired, not for the sake of others, but *solely* for the sake of God. We strive to give back to Him what He first and perfectly has given to us, by being like Him in all ways.[297]

Humility is the virtue which makes all others possible, for even the Trinity's charity is meted out to us through the humility of the Second Person. As mentioned earlier, Augustine notes the placement of humility first among the beatitudes. Humility is primary because its opposite, pride, caused Adam's declension from God. Adam, who had been the first to enjoy perfect unity with God, by succumbing to "self-concerned pride" did not seek unity, but dominance over God, thereby losing unity. He also lost true affection for the charity of God, thus he fell far from God. We who inherited Adam's sin, perpetuate it "when from a self-concerned pride a false unity is loved in part."[298]

Augustine cries out to God: "Return to You is along the path of devout humility."[299] When we find enjoyment in God, apart from our own desires, we experience true joy within, for thereby God, who is the object of our devotions, rests in our souls. With

His life — grace — in us, we live in union with Him. Self-emptying love *for* the Trinity, springing *from* the Trinity, fills the heart to
overflowing. His sufficiency completes our lack: This is humility,
to abandon all so as to gain *all*. Drawing upon the words of St.
Paul, Augustine charges us to be humble:

> 'Serve God with fear, and rejoice in Him with trem-
> bling, lest God be angry, and you perish from the right
> way' (Ps 2:11-12). Notice that he does not say, 'lest you
> fail to come to the right way,' but, 'lest you perish from
> the right way.' His point is to warn those who are walk-
> ing the right way to serve God in fear, that is, 'be not
> high-minded, but fear' (Rm 11:20). This means that
> they are not to be proud, but humble, as he elsewhere
> says: 'Do not set your mind on high things, but con-
> descend to the lowly' (Rm 12:16). Let them rejoice in
> God, but with trembling, boasting of nothing, since
> nothing is ours.[300]

The humble heart in service to God accomplishes all good
works with no regard for temporal rewards. In this way, the heart
is cleansed to obtain its heavenly reward. Sadly, the double heart
is contaminated, so that the eye of the heart perceives a phantom
of the happy life. Striving after falsehood, the soul's virtues are as
vices, even though their outward signs, such as almsgiving, may
appear true in plain sight. Augustine repeats our Lord's warning
"that we should not only beware of giving an alms motivated solely by desire for temporal things; but that in this work we are also
not to regard God in such a manner as to involve a blending or
uniting with a grasping after external interests. For here there is a
question of cleansing the heart, which, unless it is a single heart,
will not be clean."[301]

The virtue of mercy is essential to keep humility in check,
for mercy is what drives us to our knees when we lapse. When we

appeal to God's mercy from a contrite heart, the double heart we confess becomes single. God's mercy becomes our own, and we act upon our neighbor with His same mercy, so that our neighbor, even if he be an enemy, sees God's virtue in us. Augustine cautions us to remember that there are no exceptions to the mercy of the single heart, for does not "our Lord extend the rule even to our enemies 'Love your enemies, do good to them that hate you'? (Mt 5:44)."[302]

Cleaving to God

Humility and mercy are the forms of faith, the expressions of hope, and the paths towards and fruits of charity. When our hearts, impelled by faith in Christ and hope in His promises, renounce self and world, we obtain simplicity of heart from the well of God's own perfect simplicity. In this way, our hearts are purified to love as He loves, with compassion and mercy absent of desire.

> Concerning the Trinity and the knowledge of God, nothing else is to be particularly considered, except what is true love, or rather what is love. For only true love may be called love, otherwise it is desire. Therefore, it is a misuse of terms to say of those who desire that they love, just as it is a misuse of terms to say of those who love that they desire. But this is true love, that while holding fast to the truth, we may live justly, and therefore, may despise everything mortal for the sake of the love of men, whereby we wish them to live justly. For in this way we can be prepared even to die with profit for our brethren, which the Lord Jesus Christ has taught us by His example.[303]

Augustine assures us that God's mercy rewards a true disciple, for "it is obvious that when we live according to God, our mind, intent on His invisible things, must be formed continuously by His eternity, truth, and love."[304] Our gaze, then, is directed heavenward, and with Augustine we pray: "Grant what I love. For I love, and this was Your gift. Grant it, Father. You truly know how to give good gifts to Your children."[305] The love of God is "the lifegiving pleasure of a pure heart."[306]

God is the heart's "face," and nothing can separate us from the Divine Countenance as long as we "think only of the face of the heart." Augustine begs us to "force, compel, press your heart to think of things divine."[307] He makes the psalmist's words his own: "But for me it is good to be near God; I have made the Lord God my refuge that I may tell of all Thy works" (Ps 73:28, *RSV*). God's work is to convey humankind to perfection in the Beatific Vision. When we cleave to Him, we progress on the way of perfection, for "truly God is good to the upright, to those who are pure in heart" (Ps 73:1, *RSV*).[308] Nothing can separate the pure heart from God's embrace (see Rm 8:38f.).[309]

> That holy man will be so single and so pure in heart, that he will not step aside from truth, either for the sake of pleasing men or with a view to avoid any of the annoyances which beset this life. Such a son ascends to *wisdom*, which is the seventh and last step and which he enjoys in peace and tranquility. For the fear of God is the beginning of wisdom (Ps 111:10). From that beginning, then, till we reach wisdom itself, our way is by the steps now desired.[310]

Preaching on the occasion of the Octave of Easter, Augustine outlines the steps to the Wisdom of Christ. Easter, he proclaims, represents eternal bliss, the Beatific Vision. Easter is the realization of God's promise to us of His constancy, our rest from the passing of days in the present life. By cleaving to the peace of Christ which passes all understanding, we will arrive at that perpetual day of perfect Wisdom where we will see and know God in His fullness and dwell in His life. "Direct your entire reason for being Christians and for carrying His name on your forehead and in your heart solely to that life which we are destined to enjoy with the angels, where there is perpetual peace, everlasting happiness, unfailing blessedness, with no anxiety, no sadness, and no death."[311]

SPIRITUAL VIRGINITY

Virginal Fecundity: Mother Mary, Mother Church

> The glory of the male sex is in the humanity of Christ;
> the glory of womanhood is in the Mother of Christ.
> The grace of Jesus Christ has worsted the wile of the
> Serpent.[312]

The first man and the first woman were bested by the Serpent when they, through pride, succumbed to his wiles. The story does not end with their personal defeat, however. Augustine was keenly aware of the consequences of our first parents' transgressions on the human race: the defilement of body, mind, and spirit through a weakened will inclined towards concupiscence and transmitted to succeeding generations through the conjugal act. This act, as the means by which corrupt nature enters the world, is the locus of concupiscence. Sexual intercourse and lust have become intertwined, and it is only through a conversion of the heart that a man and a woman, themselves born in sin, are able to give glory to God through procreation—though not completely, and they cannot spare their offspring from their own sinful inheritance.[313]

As through a man and a woman sin and death came into the world, so through a man and a woman, redemption and life entered the world. That our defilement may be cleansed, the Son of Man was born of a woman; however, He did not subject Himself to conception through the defiled means by which sin enters the world. The Son of Man's miraculous birth from a virgin imparts to sinners the promise of *rebirth* in purity of spirit. All who belong to Christ are born spiritually of a virgin, through His bride and our mother, the Catholic Church.[314]

The circumstance of the Savior's miraculous virgin birth holds the key to the cleansing of our hearts in preparation for the Beatific Vision, and our Lord bestows this key through the pure heart of His mother, Mary. Augustine taught the perpetual virginity of Mary; whereby, her immaculate estate was in no way violated by the conception and birth of her Son, Jesus. She was not simply physically pure, but more importantly, she was spiritually blamelessness. She was born without sin, and by faith she freely vowed her obedience and consecrated her virginity, even before the angel appeared to her bearing the Trinity's request of her maternal gift to the Son. Augustine lauds Mary's faith above all: "Thus, Mary was more blessed in accepting the faith of Christ than in conceiving the flesh of Christ.... Her maternal relationship would have done Mary no good unless she had borne Christ more happily in her heart than in her flesh."[315] Her faith and purity signify the truth that only the pure in heart can carry Christ within. Indeed, Mary's *fiat* is the key to Christ; whereby, we make our own her "yes" to the Father's will in all things.[316]

Mary is far greater than model of the godly life. She is truly spiritual mother of the Church. As Christ is the Head of His body, the Church, so His mother, Mary, is His Church's mother, too. Augustine proclaims: "Indeed, she is Mother of the Head Himself in the body."[317] As an individual becomes her Son's brother or sister through Baptism into the Catholic Church, so Mary becomes mother to each of His members. When she conferred her flesh to Christ through His conception by the power of the Holy Spirit, she became His mother both in body and spirit, and our mother in spirit. Through her maternal devotion to her spiritual children, she imparts the charity of the Holy Trinity, which she carried within her womb and holds eternally in the core of her pure heart. Augustine queries:

> "'Who is my mother, or who are my brethren?' Stretching forth His hand over His disciples, He said: 'These are my brethren; and whoever does the will of my Father, he is my brother and mother and sister'" (Mt 12:48-50). What else was He teaching us except to prefer our spiritual kinship to carnal affinity, and that men are not blessed by being connected with just and holy people through blood relationship, but by being united to them through obedience to their teaching and imitation of life?[318]

Mary's fecundity as virgin is unsurpassed. By her undefiled faith in the love of God, she was the birth canal through which the Word became flesh. As mother of Christ —the Way, the Truth, and the Life — she is mother of all those who follow the Way by humility, seek the Truth in faith, and come to eternal Life through purity of heart. She is the womb of the Church, into whom her spiritual children are born anew sacramentally in the waters of Baptism. At the bosom of the fecund virgin (Mother Church and Mother Mary), we are nourished by Christ, the Son, Brother, Bridegroom, and Head.[319]

The Better Part: Lady Continence

The glory of woman and the glory of man lay in their continence, for it was their purity of heart — the man as God and the woman as His chaste and obedient handmaid —which crushed the Serpent. Everywhere and at all times, our Lord calls us to respond as His mother did, in faith, that with Him nothing is impossible: "Behold, I am the handmaid of the Lord; let it be to me according to Your word" (Lk 1:38, *RSV*). The more closely we imitate Mary's unreserved charity, the more fully we embody the glory of man and woman.[320]

The unity of spiritual and physical purity in Christ and Mary signifies the sublime charity of the Trinity; God grants Lady Continence the better part. Augustine cherishes virginity as the highest calling among sinful humanity, for the eye of the heart is sharpest where there exists perfect congruence between interior and exterior chastity. Truly, the lives of these chaste men and women are the most vivid living foretastes of the Beatific Vision. The Church, through which all the faithful receive a foretaste of the heavenly feast to come, is sanctified more fully by the presence of consecrated virgins. Augustine avers: "Since the whole Church is holy, both in body and in spirit, yet is not exclusively a virgin in body, but only in spirit, how much more holy is she in those members where she is a virgin both in body and in spirit."[321]

The form of the Church is virginity, after Christ and His spotless Mother. Each of her members is called to embrace this chastity through spiritual virginity; however, those who also are virgin in body, have chosen the superior portion. They have cause for the highest celebration, for they build up treasure in heaven for all.

> The only-begotten Son of God deigned to take upon Himself a human nature drawn from a Virgin so that He might thus link a spotless Church to Himself, its spotless Founder. In doing so He not only thought of virgins undefiled in body, but He also desired that, in that Church which the Apostle Paul calls a virgin, the minds of all should be undefiled. 'For I betrothed you to one spouse, that I might present you a chaste virgin to Christ' (2 Cor 11:2). The Church, therefore, imitating the Mother of her Lord in mind, though not in body, is both mother and virgin. Since the virginity of His Mother was in no way violated in the birth of

Christ, He likewise made His Church a virgin by ransoming her from the fornication of demons. You holy virgins, born of her undefiled virginity, who, scorning earthly nuptials, have chosen to be virgins in the flesh, rejoice now and celebrate with all solemnity the fecundity of the Virgin on this day.[322]

Virginity, consecrated to Christ in faith, is especially preferred in this time of tribulation, where we are tempted on every corner to meditate on lesser goods with the passion reserved for the greatest Good. Indeed, Augustine argues, those who are married are even more heavily burdened by life's necessities than their bodily chaste neighbors. In the present tribulation, married love is replete with obstacles to the fullness of sanctity: caring for spouse, children, and home. There is no escape from these daily trials emanating from sensual affections; however, if they are suffered for the sake of Christ, they work towards the cleansing of the heart which avails to the vision of God. In this way, marriage is a good; however, perpetual virginity, from which marriage's peculiar burdens and difficulties are absent, is to be preferred (see 1 Cor 7:28). Not even the fecundity of the married estate can compare with the virginal integrity of body and soul, whose offspring is undisturbed single-minded devotion to God. Augustine lauds holy virginity as an "angelic" lot[323]:

> Let spouses have their blessing, not because they beget children, but because they beget them honorably and lawfully and chastely and for society, and bring up their offspring rightly, wholesomely, and with perseverance; because they keep conjugal fidelity with each other; because they do not desecrate the sacrament of matrimony.
> These, however, are all duties of a human office, but virginal integrity and freedom from all carnal relation

through holy chastity is an angelic lot, and a foretaste in the corruptible flesh of perpetual incorruption. Let all carnal fecundity and all conjugal chastity bow to this. The former is not within one's own power, the latter is not found in eternity; free choice does not control carnal fecundity, heaven does not contain conjugal chastity (see Mt 22:30).[324]

Some wonder what would happen to the world if all people relinquished conjugal relations. Augustine responds that the death of the human race would be a great blessing for those who long for the vision of God. He sighs: "Would that all men had this wish, if only in 'charity, from a pure heart and a good conscience and faith unfeigned' (1 Tm 1:5). Much more quickly would the city of God be filled and the end of time be hastened."[325]

Augustine's hope is tempered by reality, however, as holy virginity is both a special gift of God's grace and a free act of the will. Not all receive this gift, and few who do respond affirmatively. Augustine pleads with those who possess self-control to abide in Lady Continence, and he counsels those who lack self-control to marry, according to the wisdom of St. Paul: "To the unmarried and the widows I say that it is well for them to remain single as I do. But if they cannot exercise self-control, they should marry. For it is better to marry than to be aflame with passion" (1 Cor 7:9, *RSV*).[326]

Holy virginity is never constrained. While there is a task associated with God's unmerited gift, the task must be accepted freely from a grateful heart, for the gift to be lived in Truth. Augustine stresses the essential liberty of virginal fidelity to Christ by drawing our attention to His Blessed Mother:

[Mary] consecrated her virginity to God while she was still ignorant of what she would conceive, so that the imitation of the heavenly life in her earthly and mortal

body might come about by vow, not by precept, by a
love of her own choice, not by the compulsion of obedience.

Thus, Christ, in being born of a virgin who, before
she knew who was to be born of her, had resolved to
remain a virgin, chose rather to approve holy virginity
than to impose it. So, even in that woman in whom
He took upon Himself the nature of a slave, He desired
virginity to be free.[327]

Those who accept God's special will of holy virginity for
their lives must possess the wisdom to know that their higher calling is, above all, *gift*, for they will be tempted to boast. Augustine greatly fears the diminishment of the virgin's dignity through
pride; whereby, one claims the gift as merit and thus one's life as
above reproach. Augustine cautions the holy virgins to forbearance through humility: "I do not say: Be like her of whom it was
said: 'Many sins are forgiven her because she has loved much' (Lk
7:47), but I fear lest, since you think that little is forgiven you,
you will love little... [that] while you glory that you will follow
the Lamb wherever He goes, you will not be able to follow Him
through the narrow ways, because of swollen pride."[328]

Virginity becomes a vice of the worst sort for the prideful.
As the call to holy virginity is the loftiest, so one who falls from
Lady Continence descends the farthest. As the virgin's body is
pure whiteness, so the eye of the heart of the prideful virgin is
blackened to all light. Augustine expresses his own mercy towards
sinners of every stripe in his caution to the holy virgin and in his
concern for the salvation of the lowliest sinner. The virgin can
express gratitude to God for this great virtue among all the virtues
and sincerely strive to obey God's commands, "yet be damned
because of the vice of pride if in his superiority he despise the
other sinners, especially those who confess their sins in prayer, or
even only in thought, since this is evident to God. Such sinners,

indeed, deserve not an arrogant upbraiding, but mercy untouched by despair."[329]

Augustine returns to humility as first among virtues, especially for the holy virgin: "'Unless you become like this child, you will not enter into the kingdom of heaven' (see Mt 18:3). Did He not praise humility most highly and place the merit of greatness in it?"[330] The majesty of the holy virgins springs from their humble vow to place the girdle of perpetual virginal chastity around them in imitation of Christ and His Blessed Mother.[331] Christ's love and humility safeguard the fidelity of their sacred vow.

> No one, therefore, protects the virginal blessing except God Himself, who bestowed it, and 'God is love' (1 Jn 4:8). Therefore, the protector of virginity is love, but the dwelling place of this protector is humility. He indeed dwells there who said that His Spirit rests upon him who is humble and peaceful and who trembles at His words (see Is 66:2).[332]

The holy virgins pledge their faithfulness to Lady Continence, not as an obedient response to God's command, for God does not command the Lady, but as an embrace of His particular request and a foretaste of the heavenly nuptial feast. They "have made themselves eunuchs for the sake of the kingdom of heaven" (Mt 19:12, *RSV*).[333] By their unity with the Divine Bridegroom in "virginity of heart and body" they glorify Him and "deservedly follow Him wherever He goes."[334] Wherever Christ, their Spouse, is found, there they are also, because His life fills their pristine hearts to capacity. They are surely blessed in this passing world, for even now they reap the first fruits of the Beatific Vision — fulfilled when God is all in all.[335]

Consecrated virgins not only reap the first fruits of their heavenly reward, they also *bear* spiritual fruits from their unspotted wombs. Augustine looks to Mary and the Church as perfect examples of the fruitfulness of holy virginity: "Mary bore the Head of this body [the Church] in the flesh; the Church bears the members of that Head in the spirit. In neither does virginity impede fecundity; in neither does fecundity destroy virginity."[336]

Augustine's presentation of virginity as fructuous stresses the rewarding, rather than sacrificial, aspect of sexual continence. The free choice of the will for the integrity of bodily and spiritual virginity is not so much a *denial* of a good of creation, but a *participation* in the crowning good of redeemed humanity. Augustine compares the offspring of the holy virgin and the holy wife to demonstrate that the one who enjoys conjugal relations, even in a spirit of holy detachment, is denied the fruit of the consecrated virgin. The married woman further suffers knowing she has brought forth eternal death in the body of her offspring until a virgin mother — the Church — brings her child, born dead through sin, to life in grace.

> Both married women of the faith and virgins consecrated to God, by holy lives and by charity 'from a pure heart and a good conscience and faith unfeigned' (1 Tm 1:5) are spiritually the mothers of Christ because they do the will of His Father. But those who, in married life, give physical birth bring forth not Christ, but Adam (see 1 Cor 15:22). They, therefore, hasten that their offspring may be initiated into the sacraments, and may become members of Christ, for they know what they have borne.[337]

The virgin in body and spirit, on the other hand, receives bountiful gifts of fructuousness and thus rejoices, for she bears the fruit of everlasting life in the midst of temporality, the peace of God which conquers sin and death.

It is your blessing, O virginal soul, that, just as you are
a virgin, thus preserving perfectly in your heart what
you are by rebirth, while preserving in your flesh what
you are by birth, you *conceive of the fear of the Lord and
bring forth the spirit of salvation.*[338]

Who else but Christ Jesus is the spirit of salvation borne
by the holy virgins? When they emptied themselves completely
for Him in purity of body and spirit, He filled them with Himself. Augustine states: "You have gained as the spouse of your
heart Him whom you could not bring forth as your child in the
flesh."[339] Yet Christ is also the child of His virgins, as well as their
spouse, for they are united with His Blessed Mother spiritually
through their chaste imitation of her. As Mary became Christ's
mother through obedience to the Father's will, so also are our
Lord's virgins His mothers because they do the will of the Father.
"For whoever does the will of my Father in heaven is my brother,
and sister, and mother" (Mt 12:50, *RSV*).

The "fear of the Lord" and the "spirit of salvation" beat within the hearts of all the holy virgins, drawing others to their sacred
breasts who long to share in their spiritual fecundity. Those who
consecrate their lives to the Bridegroom through Lady Continence
are the virgins' offspring; thus their fruits bear witness to the truth
that the holy virgins have chosen the better part.

That virgin, therefore, is rightly preferred to the married woman, who neither places herself before the multitude to be loved, while she is seeking the love of one
out of the multitude, nor unites herself to one already
found, concerned with 'the things of the world, how
she may please her husband' (1 Cor 7:34) but who so
loves Him who is 'beautiful above the sons of men' (Ps
44:3) that, since she cannot, like Mary, conceive Him
in the flesh, she preserves even her body intact for Him
who has been conceived in her heart.[340]

The Good of Marriage: Spiritual Virginity

Few of the faithful imitate Christ's holy virginity, although this calling is certainly the highest. Augustine consoles the vast multitudes who have not chosen that extraordinary path of blessedness. While it is true these souls will never bear the integrity of bodily and spiritual continence, they may yet be blessed through spiritual virginity. Their hearts are cleansed by their single-minded devotion to God and imitation of His charity; thus when they meet the Lord face to face they will be as spotless brides.[341]

Though not virgins in body, the married and the widowed are invited to sit at the feet of the holy virgins and rejoice in their blessings. There they will learn the virgin's detachment from all the goods of creation; they will delight in the fruits of Lady Continence; they will gain the humility and submissive obedience which became the *fiat* of our Mother, Mary; they will grow strong in spirit from bearing the inescapable sufferings accompanying marriage and the rearing of children; finally, they will purify their hearts as they lift affections above the carnal to the spiritual plane. While they cannot lay claim to the unequalled merits of the holy virgins, they may cherish the particular goods God bestows upon the married estate: "offspring, fidelity, sacrament."[342] Augustine states: "Marriage, therefore, is a good in which the married are better in proportion as they fear God more chastely and more faithfully, especially if they also nourish spiritually the children whom they desire carnally."[343] What God gives, He hallows; thus marriage and its fruits are sanctified for the sake of His glory.[344]

Married people encounter their most formidable challenge to spiritual continence in their task to squelch the temptations of the flesh. Sexual intercourse is the locus of concupiscence because it is nearly impossible to remove lust from the conjugal act. Augustine expresses this lamentable condition; whereby, concupiscence has horribly lessened the good of procreation that God conferred upon Adam and Eve. Evil, which is a declension from the good, attacks the procreative act with a vengeance.[345]

The generative intimacy shared between the man and the woman according to God's purpose, is a great good; however, in the present life, the very manner of generating offspring has become disfigured as a consequence of the Fall. This side of Paradise, the conjugal act never will be fully restored, although when a married couple accomplishes it solely for the purpose of producing offspring, it becomes a good, albeit a far lesser good.[346]

Augustine counsels married people to cultivate continence of the soul, for by virtue of their estate, they do not enjoy continence of the body. This virtue is so great as to change the relationship between mind and body; whereas, the heart's affinity for the passions of the flesh are replaced by the interior longing to bear Christ's holy passion. The first step to cleansing the heart is to refrain from marital relations except for the purposes of procreation. This restraint is a daily struggle for those who have tasted the pleasures of marital relations. Augustine offers comfort to the afflicted by explaining that God readily extends His merciful forgiveness to the husband and wife who, sincerely striving for this goal, occasionally fail.[347]

For those who are married, continence is formed as "the disposition of the souls, to be shown... in practice in accord with the opportunity of the time and circumstances."[348] In this manner, husband and wife may live holy continence within conjugal chastity. They bear the fruits of marriage — children and charity — through their conjugal love. They purify their hearts as they love each other for God's sake, placing Him above all, thus in their affections they become spiritually blameless. If the eye of the heart is without blemish, the sanctity of the body will resist defilement.[349]

"'Stop your ears to your impure members on earth, and mortify them.' They declare delights to you, but 'not in accord with the law of the Lord your God' (Ps 118:85). This debate in my heart was a struggle of myself against myself."[350] With these words, Augustine threw down the gauntlet of Lady Continence in

his own life. Being of the same mind for the married faithful in
his charge, he challenges them to extended periods of sexual continence, for such acts of mortification work towards the integrity of
chastity in body and spirit. When the hearts of husband and wife
develop a spirit of detachment from worldly affections, they reflect
the true grace of the sacrament. Augustine asks married persons
to meditate on the incomparable matrimony of Mary and Joseph
who shared unsurpassed conjugal love. Their restraint from the
marital act did not preclude a true marriage. On the contrary, the
integrity of chastity in body, mind, and spirit which they shared,
provided a fitting home for the Son of Man. Their marriage stands
as the crowning glory of all nuptial unions. Augustine begs married persons to strive for sexual continence after the union of our
Blessed Mother and St. Joseph, her chaste spouse, that they may
purify themselves in readiness for the heavenly banquet.[351]

Sexual continence within marriage requires heroic virtue,
but all things are possible with God: "'I can do all things in Him
who strengthens me' (Ph 4:11-12)."[352] Indeed, one can be spiritually chaste as God commands; one also can be sexually continent
through the free choice of the will and by God's grace, for "'none
can be continent unless You grant it' (Ws 8:21)."[353] Augustine
raises a prayer of hope to God, the author of all blessings:

> My entire hope is exclusively in Your very great mercy.
> Grant what You command, and command what You
> will. You require continence....: 'As I knew that no one
> can be continent except God grants it, and this very
> thing is part of wisdom, to know whose gift this is.' By
> continence we are collected together and brought to the
> unity from which we disintegrated into multiplicity. He
> loves You less who together with You loves something
> which he does not love for Your sake. O love, You ever
> burn and are never extinguished. O charity, my God,

set me on fire. You command continence; grant what
You command, and command what You will.[354]

Heroic virtue requires extreme humility. Augustine is acutely aware of the incalculable distance that exists between God and
humanity. The more we sin, the farther we fall. Exalting oneself in
a false imitation of God only widens the chasm. Instead, we grow
closer to the exalted Trinity as we submit to the humble likeness
of the Son of Man. If upon our death Christ finds we have made
our earthly home in His Way of the Cross — His poverty, humiliation, suffering, compassion, mercy, and continence — He will
make a grand home for us at the right hand of His throne of glory.
Augustine cries out: "Lord my God, How deep is Your profound
mystery, and how far away from it have I been thrust by the consequences of my sins.... How exalted You are, and the humble in
heart are Your house (Ps 137:6; 145:8). You lift up those who are
cast down (Ps 144:14; 145:8), and those whom You raise to that
summit which is Yourself do not fall."[355]

The disposition of continence within the soul is the training
ground for purity of heart, without which the vision of God is a
fleeting wish. Augustine extends a sobering warning to the faithful that we are in mortal combat with the powers of the world for
the life of the soul. Our adversary is the Devil, a formidable foe.
Augustine queries how it can be possible to conquer this invisible enemy. St. Paul shows us the way: "'Freeing Himself of His
body, [Christ] made an example of the principalities and powers,
confidently triumphing over them within Himself' (Col 2:15).
Consequently, when invisible and sinful desires are overcome, we
then overcome the unseen power of our enemy. Hence, by overcoming within ourselves the inordinate love for things temporal,
we are necessarily, within ourselves, overcoming him also who
rules within man by those sinful desires."[356] Within marriage,
the greatest challenge for husband and wife in their battle for the

disposition of holy continence in their souls, is to overcome inordinate affections, one for the other, and both for their children. When their love for God, alone, becomes their ground of joy, their familial love is transformed into an expression of the love of the Holy Trinity.[357]

6

Means to Purity of Heart

God: Source and Summit

'Let us make man to our image and likeness' (Gn 1:26). We believe that man has been made in the image of the Trinity.... John the Apostle says: 'We shall be like Him, for we shall see Him just as He is'; because he, too, spoke of Him (i.e., of God the Trinity) of whom he had said: 'We are the children of God' (1 Jn 3:2). And the immortality of the flesh will be perfected at that moment of the resurrection of which the Apostle Paul says: 'In the twinkling of an eye, at the last trumpet, and the dead shall rise again incorruptible; and we shall be changed' (see 1 Cor 15:52). For in the very twinkling of an eye, before the judgment, which will rise in power, incorruption, and glory as a spiritual body, which is now sown in weakness, corruption and dishonor as a natural body. But the image which is being renewed day by day in the spirit of the mind and in the knowledge of God, not outwardly, but inwardly, will be perfected by the vision itself which will then be after the judgment face to face, but it is

121

making progress towards it now 'through a mirror in an obscure manner' (1 Cor 13:12).[358]

God created us in His image of perfect charity, wisdom and beauty, endowing us with the clarity of vision to behold His loveliness face to face and to be happy with Him forever.[359] By our first parents' fall through pride, however, we disfigured our image, obscured our vision, and abandoned our happy home. Pride is the root of all evil, the self-inflicted disease that weakens our will and corrupts our nature. Pride is a tenacious foe and a jealous mistress: When the will makes the slightest movement away from the self, pride snatches it back. Pride is easily deluded into thinking it is truth when at times throughout life, abundance, successes, and joys ease the pain of want, failures, trials, and tribulations. When these pleasures inevitably fail, however, the will must choose one of two paths: to continue in pride unto despair or to admit weakness and humbly turn to God.[360]

God alone can restore what we have undone. How do we acquire the Master's restorative powers? Augustine answers that we must flee the self and enter God. "Your *words* stuck fast in my heart and on all sides I was defended by you. Of your eternal life I was certain, though I saw it 'in an enigma and as if in a mirror' (1 Cor 13:12). All doubt had been taken from me that there is an indestructible substance from which comes all substance. My desire was not to be certain of You but to be more stable in You."[361]

God's divine providence is His Word. This is the creative Word which brings all things into being, "the constant cause of inconstant things."[362] This Word, in an act of utmost charity, surrendered constancy up to inconstancy: "And the Word became flesh and dwelt among us" (Jn 1:14, *RSV*). Augustine asks: "What more could have been done for our salvation?"[363] God's providence is His superabundant compassion for the heart which is "aroused in the love of Your mercy and the sweetness of Your grace."[364] Instead of abandoning us to our just deserts, He entered into us to rescue us from our self-imposed exile and death. The incarnation of the Son of God brought God's life into the human being again. What else is His life, but grace? His gift of Self — His humble life, His dolorous passion, His ignoble death, and His glorious resurrection — brought us invincible life. The Father, through the gift of the Son, adopted orphaned humanity and hallowed us by His Holy Spirit.[365]

God's charity made manifest in the self-emptying of the Word-made-flesh, is the restorative balm of our wounded nature. Out of divine charity, Christ gave up His Spirit that we may have His Spirit in us. "'Love is diffused in our hearts by the Holy Spirit who is given to us' (Rm 5:5). Concerning the things of the Spirit [St. Paul] demonstrates that the way of charity is 'supereminent' (1 Cor 12:1)... that we may know 'the supereminent knowledge of the love of Christ' (Eph 3:14, 19)."[366] When God *graces* us with His love we grow in the image and likeness of Him: His image of purity and His likeness of charity.

The way of Divine Providence is a mystery, the mystery of being in the face of nothingness. Moved by God's grace, the will, teetering on the precipice between being and nothingness, chooses being. Divine Providence rescues the will from the snatches of death and sets the will on the path towards life — His own life. The road to the fullness of being, fraught with a plethora of seeming paradoxes, is a mystery of faith: We must die to live; we must become nothing to possess fullness of life. We must forfeit our image of the self in order to don the image of God. We must sorrow to reap joy. We must lose the affections of the heart to gain the charity of God. We must become foolish to obtain wisdom. We must assume the yoke of slavery to enjoy freedom. We must be weak to develop strength. We must be submissive to be exalted. We must die to be born. We must leave ourselves behind to be where He is, while at the same time enter ourselves to find Him. We must lose ourselves to discover Him that we may gain ourselves where He is found.[367] Augustine cries out:

How shall I call upon my God, my God and Lord? Surely when I call on Him, I am calling on Him to come into me…. I would have no being; I would not have any existence, unless You were in me. Or rather, I would have no being if I were not in You 'of whom are all things, through whom are all things, in whom are all things' (Rm 11:36).

You are not scattered but reassemble us. In filling all things, You fill them all with the whole of Yourself.[368]

"And the Word became flesh and dwelt among us, *full of grace and truth*; we have beheld His glory, glory as of the only Son from the Father" (Jn 1:14, *RSV*). We derive our being from the fullness of His grace, according to the sanctity of our souls. We behold His glory with the heavenward eyes of a pure heart: "Whoever, then, has Christ in his heart, so that no earthly or temporal thing — not even those that are legitimate and allowed — are preferred to Him, has Christ as a foundation."[369]

The Church: Life of the Body

For the Church is His body… even His spouse (Rv 19:7; 21:9)…. He holds together in the bond of unity and love, which is its true health. Moreover He exercises it in the present time, and purges it with many wholesome afflictions, that when He has transplanted it from this world to the eternal world, He may take it to Himself as His bride, without spot or wrinkle, or any such thing.[370]

Augustine cherishes the Catholic Church as Christ's greatest gift to us, for our Master is found within her; therefore, if we want to be where He is, we must make our earthly abode in His Church. Augustine confesses she is his sufficiency. We enter heaven's gates in time through her ministrations; whereby, Christ breaks into our world, especially through the reception of the sacraments. His Spirit sanctifies us, and His Body and Blood nourish us. Fed on the pure food of grace, we may become one with Him in perfect unity.[371]

The Church is where we *touch* God. Augustine expounds on the meaning of Jesus' words to Mary Magdalene when she sought His dead body in the tomb and, finding Him alive, longed for His embrace. "Do not hold me, for I have not yet ascended to my Father" (Jn 20:17, *RSV*). Augustine explains the deeper meaning of Christ's admonition: We can only touch the *ascended* Christ. But how can it be, Augustine wonders, that we can touch Christ in heaven if we cannot touch Him on earth? The answer lies in faith: We touch Him on earth through belief in Him. We touch Him by faith now, that we may hold fast to Him in His heavenly kingdom. "The touch, moreover, signifies belief; he who believes in Christ touches Christ."[372]

Augustine leads us to the woman suffering from a hemorrhage for twelve years as an exemplar of the faith. She believed to touch Him meant salvation. "If I only touch His garment, I shall be made well" (Mt 9:21, *RSV*). She longed to be saved of her bodily affliction, but His touch healed her *completely*. The health of the soul is what matters, for Augustine preaches:

> Then, so that we might know the real significance of touching Him, immediately the Lord said to His disciples: "'Who touched me?' They answered: 'The crowds press upon You, and do You say, "Who touched me?"'" And He replied: 'Someone touched me'" (Lk 8:45-46), as if to say: *'The crowd presses; but faith touches.'* Hence, Mary Magdalene... seems to represent the Church when He had ascended into heaven.[373]

The Church is the figurative representative of Mary Magdalene. The Church touches by belief, and she metes out that touch to her members through the means of grace. If we want to touch heaven on earth, we must be in the body of which He is the Head. Outside Mother Church, there is no faith — no touch of salvation.[374] The Sacrament of Baptism is our entrance way into the Church, with each sacrament conveying Christ's particular means of sanctifying grace, ordained by Him for the salvation of souls. "When the goodness and loving kindness of God our Savior appeared, He saved us, not because of deeds done by us in righteousness, but in virtue of His own mercy, by the washing of regeneration and renewal in the Holy Spirit" (Tt 3:5, *RSV*). Baptism, by removing the stain of original sin, is the first and necessary step towards the cleansing of the heart. In the sacrament, it is not a solitary priest of his own power remitting sin, but Christ Himself, in the person of the priest, through the form of His body, the Church.[375]

Once baptized, the renewal commences. Baptism brings hope through the remission of sins and sanctification by grace. The cleansing of the heart through this initial sacrament prepares and fortifies the weak will to submit to the will of God. This is the way of perfection of both spirit and body. Although the body decays and dies, if the pure heart brings the flesh into submission through a chaste life, that body becomes a perfect offering, along with a pristine heart, to God. "So, we do not lose heart. Though our outer nature is wasting away, our inner nature is being renewed every day" (2 Cor 4:16, *RSV*). Augustine reiterates St. Paul's message of hope:

> Whoever, then, is being renewed in the knowledge of God, and in justice and holiness of truth, by making progress day by day, transfers his love from temporal to eternal things, from visible to intelligible things, from carnal to spiritual things, and constantly endeavors to restrain and to lessen the desire for the former, and to bind himself by love to the latter. But he does so in

proportion to the divine help that he receives, for the saying of God is: 'Without me you can do nothing' (Jn 15:5).

If the last day of this life shall find anyone in such progress and growth holding fast to the faith of the Mediator, he will be received by the holy angels, in order that he may be brought to the God whom he has worshipped, and by whom he is to be brought to perfection; and at the end of the world he shall receive an incorruptible body, not for punishment but for glory. For the likeness to God in this image will then be perfect. The Apostle Paul says of this vision: 'We now see through a mirror in an obscure manner, but then face to face' (1 Cor 13:12). He likewise says: 'But we, beholding the glory of the Lord with face unveiled, are transformed into the same image from glory to glory, as through the Spirit of the Lord' (2 Cor 3:18). This is what takes place in those who are making progress steadily day by day.[376]

One must be within Christ's body, the Church, to obtain the sure hope of the Beatific Vision. By the power of God, through His Church, we are healed of the disease of original sin, and set on the path towards salvation. The ordinary manner of baptizing is through the priests; however, according to God's mercy, the Church allows for Baptism by the extraordinary means of desire, especially through the blood of the martyrs or the earnest longing expressed in the heart of one on the threshold of mortal death. Augustine declares: "For whatever unbaptized persons die confessing Christ, this confession is of the same efficacy for the remission of sins as if they were washed in the sacred font of Baptism."[377]

All the sacraments nourish us on our journey, such as the sacrament of the remission of sins, instituted by Christ in His commission to the Church to bind and loose. None, however, affords a more direct "touch" of our ascended Savior than the Sacrament of the Eucharist. We see, touch, and taste Christ in the breaking of the bread. Augustine tells us there is no surer consolation for us who are far from Christ in the body than the *nearness* of His Body: We approach the holy altar with a purified heart through the remission of sins, and we depart the altar with hearts illuminated with the presence of Christ's own Body and Blood *in us*. "He did not wish to be recognized except in [the breaking of the bread], for the sake of us who were not destined to see Him in the flesh but who, nevertheless, would eat His flesh… let the breaking of bread bring consolation to you. The absence of the Lord is not real absence; have faith, and He whom you do not see is with you."[378]

Although the sacraments are the necessary means of grace, the Church, as Christ's Body, hallows our lives in countless other ways as well: the consensus of the Magisterium, the unbroken see of Peter; the trust of the faithful, the proof of miracles; the deepening of faith, hope, and charity in the lives of the faithful through prayer, fasting, and almsgiving; the enlightening of the mind through doctrine and the record of truth that is Scripture; finally, the name, itself, *catholica*, which belongs to Christ's Church and none other. She sanctifies us with God's grace for our redemption: "The Church's faith is taught in very few words. In it eternal truths are proposed which cannot yet be grasped by the carnal-minded; also deeds of past and future time, which God in His eternal providence has accomplished and will accomplish for the salvation of men."[379]

Indeed, the Church is our Lord's depositor of truth and the sanctifier of souls whose minds and hearts have been contaminated by sins. It is then necessary that the Church be chaste, our Virgin Mother in spirit, for it is by the chaste love of her Head — Himself born of a holy Virgin — that we are redeemed. The happy life is rewarded to those who, within the bosom of Mother Church, conform to the life and love of her Head. Augustine instructs: "For to Christians, this rule of life is given, that we should love the Lord our God with all the heart, with all the soul, and with all the mind, and our neighbor as ourselves; for on these two commandments land all the law and the prophets. Rightly, then, the Catholic Church, most true mother of Christians, does thou not only teach that God alone, to find whom is the happiest life, must be worshipped in perfect purity and chastity?"[380] Scripture, the sacraments, and prayer are the tools Mother Church employs in the training and rearing of her children in chastity, that we may present this priceless dowry to our most chaste Bridegroom, for the nuptial feast — the Beatific Vision — is reserved for the pure in heart.[381]

The Canon of Scripture

> [It] is difficult to contemplate and to comprehend fully the substance of God, which makes changeable things without any change in itself, and creates temporal things without any temporal movement of its own. Therefore, the purification of our soul is necessary in order that it may be able to see that ineffable thing in an ineffable manner. Since we have not as yet become endowed with this, we are strengthened by faith and are led along more accessible roads, in order that we may gain the proficiency and skill to grasp that reality…. 'And I, brethren, could not speak to you as spiritual men but only as carnal; as to little ones in Christ, I gave you milk to drink not food, for you were not yet able, but neither indeed are you still able' (1 Cor 3:1-2).[382]

The Scripture is Mother Church's invaluable tool of instruction. By it, she teaches her children the path to purity of heart and righteous actions. The text is the superlative instrument of learning, from which no one tires, no matter one's location near or far from God: from the uninitiated, to the newborn in the faith, through the mature, pristine soul. The Word which entices the babe in the faith is also fullness to the wise heart. Augustine determines Scripture's purpose is "to arouse the affections of the weak, so that by means of them, as though they were steps, they may mount to higher things according to their own modest capacity and abandon the lower things.... 'Every good gift and every perfect gift is from above, coming down from the Father of lights with whom there is no change or shadow of movement' (Jm 1:17)."[383] Scripture leads the way to happiness; it teaches the essential truths for the beatification of the soul. The eye of the heart is cleansed to see God by believing everything therein with the mind, cleaving to these truths with the heart, and conforming to its precepts according to an upright will.[384]

Scripture anticipates the Beatific Vision within the constraints of time. The past events which Scripture relates prefigure the Trinity's pledge of the future. When we read of the past in God's holy writ, we learn the ways of God's constancy, that is, His timeless charity within temporality that we may live in His love eternally. His Word is witness to the kind of people we had been, are now, and will become by His power and love, manifested in the Father's mighty deeds and in the Son's abject weakness. "God, Himself, is the one End of the soul's striving."[385]

Our hearts are changed, Augustine proclaims, when we take God's Word to heart. When we uphold the purity of the Lord's doctrines, both our knowledge and our affections are purified. The mind is cleansed to know God; the heart is purified to love Him; the eye is sharpened to see Him, now in part but then in all His glory.

> Scripture enjoins nothing except charity, and condemns
> nothing except lust, and in that way fashions the lives
> of men.... Scripture asserts nothing but the Catholic

faith, in regard to things past, future, and present. It is a narrative of the past, a prophecy of the future, and a description of the present. But all these tend to nourish and strengthen charity, and to overcome and root out lust.[386]

Augustine maintains that the merits of God's holy writ are reserved for those in the Catholic Church, for the Scripture is canonical. It is the highest authority of God's Word spoken from the mouths of the Old Testament prophets and the New Testament Apostles. The wisdom and jurisdiction of the Church convey the harmony of both testaments in her explication of divine revelation and binding moral precepts for the living out of the gospels. When we read or listen to Scripture under the protective mantle of the Catholic faith, assenting to every inerrant word without exception, we avail our hearts of the sacred text's purgative remedies. The Word of God is a healing balm for our sin-sick hearts, excising the fatal wound of our past and growing in strength and vigor of faith in the present, so in the future our hearts will be found worthy of the glory of God.[387]

Prayer, Fasting, and Almsgiving

The worship of God in prayer is an invaluable aid to our growth in holiness. Prayer gives God His due, saying in various and many ways that we believe God's Word is true. Whether our prayers are formed in words, ideas, or sentiments, on the altar in the rites of the Church, or by our actions, our prayers assent to the teachings of God in Christ. The richness of the means and forms of prayer attests to the splendor of the faith; whereby, our Lord attends to the stirrings of the heart towards Him according to the uniqueness of each person, as well as the commonality of the body in the rites and corporate prayers of the Church.[388]

The nature of prayer is the conversion of the heart to single-minded love of God. The reason for prayer is to condition the soul for the reception of grace, as prayer is both a means of grace and its consequence. Prayer is the poultice applied to the heart wounded by sin, administering slow, sure, and steady healing. Prayer functions as a weapon in mortal combat, and its aim is true. The evil foe is vanquished, not with power and might, but with supplications and praise on the lips of a humble heart. Prayer is the touch of God to humanity, the divine embrace between heaven and earth.[389]

Augustine confesses we "humiliate our souls by prayer."[390] The very act of prayer is a renunciation of pride, for prayer is a confession of our need and a turning towards the wholly Other for satisfaction. Shedding all pretenses of self-reliance and strength, we come as it were naked before God. Prayer is a superlative act of intimacy: the self-emptying of our hearts to be filled by Him. We pray: "Thy kingdom come, Thy will be done" (Mt 6:10, *RSV*) —unto my heart. In this way, prayer is both praise and supplication.

When we petition God to receive small goods in time, such as consolation in grief, cure of an illness, grace for a loved one, pacification of anxiety over daily trials, victory in battle, etc., we are asking for happiness. The joy we seek in little things is rooted in a heart which yearns for joy above all. This is the joy which endures in the midst of sorrow now and will be absent of sorrow in the Beatific Vision.

Augustine maintains there is no contradiction between God's persevering will and prayer's efficaciousness. Prayer is a God-ordained work for the purpose of the purification of the heart. Although God foreknows our needs and His providential acts for the benefit of souls, He nevertheless blesses the prayerful heart with His grace. The heart, then, shares in His peace and purity and is fashioned into a worthy receptacle of His munificence.[391] Augustine explains this beautiful transformation of the "inner eye" of the heart through prayers:

[Every] effort we make in praying calms the heart, makes it clean, and renders it more capable of receiving the divine gifts which are poured upon us in a spiritual manner.... But we are not always prepared to receive, attracted as we are to other things and unenlightened by our desire for temporal things. Hence there takes place in prayer a turning of the heart to Him who is ever ready to give if we will but accept what He gives. *And in this turning there is effected a cleansing of the inner eye*, consisting in the exclusion of those things which filled our earth-bound desires *so that the vision of a pure heart may be able to bear the pure light*, radiating from God without any diminution or setting; and not only to bear it, but also to remain in it, not merely without discomfort but with the unspeakable joy whereby truly and unequivocally a blessed life is perfected.[392]

Augustine draws us to Scripture, especially to Christ's own instructions, on the correct way to pray. "'Enter into your chambers' (Mt 6:6). What are these 'chambers' but the hearts themselves."[393] Our Lord instructs us to leave the world behind in the inner recesses of the heart, for seclusion from the world's temptations is eminently necessary for prayer; otherwise, our hearts will become so crowded as to drive our Lord away for lack of room. When Augustine speaks about entering our chambers, he is speaking literally, as well as figuratively. When possible, withdraw into a place in the farthest reaches of the heart where prayer is offered in secret. Our Lord's rules for prayer, Augustine declares, are "for the cleansing of the heart, and the only thing that makes the heart clean is the undivided and single-minded striving after eternal life from pure love of wisdom alone."[394]

Augustine suggests we use an economy of words in prayer, according to the example of our Lord's prayer to His Father in heaven, which expresses perfect trust in God's promises and unconditional abandonment to Divine Providence. When we offer His simple yet supremely profound prayer, we continue the cleansing of our hearts begun at Baptism. The moment we begin: *Our Father, which art in heaven*, we thrust ourselves on the constant mercy of God, who ever answers the heartfelt cries of His people.[395]

Almsgiving, which includes fasting and "almsdeeds," is tethered to prayer. Augustine calls these two types of beneficent love "giving and forgiving."[396] Fasting and almsgiving are concrete purgative acts of mind and body, which unite with contemplative prayer to effect the integrity of continence in all faculties. When we fast and give alms we recall our own want to be filled by God. As fasting suppresses the appetites, it aids the chastening of the body along with the spirit. In the same way, almsgiving checks the lower desires through unselfish giving to those in material or spiritual need. Fasting and almsgiving, if done for the sake of God, unburden the heart of temporal concerns; thus absent of distractions, the heart becomes single.[397] The heart must be single, therefore, to bear the luminescence of the *One* God. The blessed heart is the heart which is illuminated by the light and also rests within its incomprehensible brilliance.[398]

While we wait for Christ to come again, we partake of His Body and Blood in the Breaking of the Bread. Until we see Christ face to face, the Eucharist is the *single* happy end of the unity of prayer, fasting, and almsgiving. It is God's gift of charity for our salvation. When we eat His Body and drink His Blood, we consume His charity, thus His charity becomes our own. We are obligated to the same life of self-emptying love for the salvation of others. Augustine, preaching on Luke 24:13-31, provides a heart-swelling testament to Christ's impassioned invitation to us to participate in His redemptive charity. Augustine's obvious single-minded devotion to God and love of neighbor in Him is moving; it is a fitting testament to the works of love of those who are pure in heart.

The disciples on the road to Emmaus heard, rejoiced, breathed freely again; as they themselves acknowledged, their hearts burned within them; yet they did not recognized the Light that was with them.

What a mystery this is, my brethren! He enters their abode, He becomes their Guest, and Him whom they did not recognize on the road they recognize in the breaking of the bread. Learn how to receive guests in whom you recognize Christ. Do you not know that, if you receive any Christian, you receive Him! Does He not say: 'I was a stranger and you took me in'? And when the reply is given: 'Lord, when did we see Thee a stranger?' He answers: 'As long as you did it for one of these, the least of my brethren, you did it for me' (Mt 25:35, 38, 40). Therefore, when Christian receives Christian, the members serve the members; and the Head rejoices and considers what was bestowed on His member as given to Himself. Here, then, let the hungry Christ be fed; let the thirsty Christ be given a drink; let the naked Christ be clothed; let the stranger Christ be sheltered; let the sick Christ be visited. The exigency of our journey makes this an obligation, for on our journey through life, we must live where Christ is in need. He is in need in His followers; of Himself He has no need. But He, who is needy in His followers and who abounds in Himself, draws all the needy to Himself.[399]

All are needy whom Christ draws to Himself, and He satiates the needs of those who possess purity of heart with His own self. Within the mystery of redemption, God requires those whom He has graced to empty themselves, so as to fill the needs of another in imitation of Christ's self-emptying charity unto death. The road to fullness of life is navigated by way of emptiness. Those who *hu-*

miliate themselves through prayer and the chastisements of fasting and almsgiving will be *exalted* forever, and even now they taste the first fruits of everlasting glory. Augustine is certain "the just can be called heaven," for so the just one is the temple of God.[400]

7

Requirement and Reward: An Organic Relationship

The Chief Good

> 'One thing I have asked of the Lord, that I may gaze upon the delight of the Lord,' and regarding which the Lord Himself declares: 'And I will love him and manifest myself to him' (Jn 14:21), and on account of which alone we purify our hearts by faith, so that we may be blessed: *'Blessed are the clean of heart for they shall see God,'* and any other things that have been said about this vision, which he who searches for with the eyes of love finds scattered with the greatest profusion through all the Scriptures—that vision alone is our supreme good, and we are commanded to do rightly whatever we do in order that we may obtain it.[401]

If we are to gaze upon God in eternity, Augustine espouses, we must gaze upon Him in temporality. We must present our hearts blessed before we are beatified. The Beatific Vision is for those who live in the present in the nearness of the Trinity. Those who offer their hearts as a living receptacle of God's charity receive the peace and joy which the world cannot give. They are happy even before they attain their heavenly reward because their lives are foretastes of the kingdom of God. "The happy life exists when that which is man's chief good is both loved and possessed."[402]

The chief good of a particular soul is the measure of its love, and the soul will reap its reward or punishment according to the object of its love. If the soul loves God reservedly through the withholding of a double heart, then the chief good of the soul is itself. Because the soul loves God less, it will fall short of the glory of God. If the soul cleaves to God singly, with all heart, soul, and mind, then nothing will separate the soul from the love of God on earth or in heaven. Augustine tells us the choice is clear: We must put all our strivings into loving God in all things such that our whole life is a thank-offering to Him. "The perfection of all our good things and our perfect good is God. We must neither come short of this nor go beyond it: the one is dangerous, the other impossible."[403]

We cannot say we love God as our chief good without showing Him the depth of our love by the way we live. All the blessed share a oneness of mind and heart. Those who possess single-minded worship of God direct every faculty towards Him. Augustine explains that we begin with the eye as "the candle of the body: If therefore your eye is single, your whole body shall be full of light."[404] When each faculty is single, all together mutually give honor to God and conform to the good intention of the upright will. In this way, even the smallest act of kindness or the simplest prayer will manifest the brilliance of God. The congruence of purity in thought, word, and deed is the requisite for eternal luminescence in the Beatific Vision.[405]

Location of Heart

The pure heart is never far from God. Augustine employs the terminology of space and location when speaking of the salvation of souls. The soul progresses towards or declines from the Beatific Vision. The path either way depends on the heart's cleanliness or decrepitude. A heart dragged down by the lure of temporal goods will one day be crushed by their weight, unable to rise aloft towards the liberty of heaven. Those who travel on a downward spiral into nonexistence bind their hearts to the fleeting goods of this world rather than to the One, *constant* Good. They seek to enjoy the beauty of God's creative goods for their own sake, rather than to use them for God's sake. Augustine is adamant on the issue of use and enjoyment: "For to enjoy a thing is to rest with satisfaction in it for its own sake."[406] Contrariwise, to use something is to "employ whatever means are at one's disposal to obtain what one desires if it is a proper object of desire; for an unlawful use ought rather to be called an abuse."[407] When we use the goods of this world as ends in themselves, they eat away at the heart, thus by corruption the soul becomes less than its own nature, less than human, as a beast. In this way, the heart's punishment is the nonexistence of the soul as God intended souls, that is, the soul suffers eternal death. While we were made in the Trinity's image and likeness, the soul that plunges into evil resembles the Trinity in nothing. As Christ said, it would be better if that person were never born. He did not say this to overturn the rightness of all God's creative acts; rather, our Lord is judging one who rejects God by an act of the will that hardens the heart to Divine Providence.

Augustine laments our sinful condition: "We have wandered far from God; and if we wish to return to our Father's home, this world must be used, not enjoyed, that so the invisible things of God may be clearly seen, being understood by the things that are made, that is, that by means of what is material and temporary we may lay hold of that which is spiritual and eternal."[408] Our spiritual and eternal good is the Supreme Good, the Blessed Trinity, and all the earth sings God's praises because He made all. When we cleave to that great truth, we will behold the Trinity's imprint in the good, the true, and the beautiful, and immediately our hearts will be drawn upwards towards the source of all goodness, truth, and beauty. Augustine confesses his transgression: "I loved beautiful things of a lower order, and I was going down to the depths."[409] Through his conversion of heart, however, he discovered the reason for the lure of the beautiful. "What is it which charms and attracts us to the things we love? It must be the grace and loveliness inherent in them, or they would in no way move us."[410] God — Father, Son, and Holy Spirit — is the One, the authentic object of our enjoyment. When we turn our hearts to Him in confession of sin and profession of faith, He responds in mercy; His grace purges the heart of past defilements and restores what was once corrupt to wholeness and fullness of life, that He may be enjoyed without interruption.[411]

"Blessed are the pure in heart, for they shall see God." Where and how shall they see the vision God has promised His own? They shall see Him with the eye of the heart enlightened by faith, and they will perceive Him where He is: both *inside* and *outside*. Augustine leads us where God resides within. "You say to me: 'Show me your God.' I answer: 'Turn your attention to your own heart for a little while.'"[412] Augustine directs us to scour the heart of all impurity out of love for God, thereby making a spotless home for Him, for so our Lord tells us: "If a man loves me, he will keep my word, and my Father will love him, and we will come to him and make our home with him" (Jn 14:23, *RSV*). The heart is the hearth of the fire of God's love.[413]

We find God in His heavenly realm. The soul which has become luminescent through purity of heart is conveyed to and rests within the utterly transcendent light of God. The soul which turns to God through conversion of heart flies to God's happy home. Here is the mystery of our heavenly abode: Where else is His happy home but in the hearts of those who love Him? Where else are the hearts of those who love Him but in His own being? He is in us insofar as we are in Him. Augustine proclaims this mystery of faith:

> O blessed creature, if there be such: happy in cleaving to Your felicity, happy to have You as eternal inhabitant and its source of light! I do not find any better name for the Lord's 'heaven of heaven' (Ps 113:16) than Your House. There Your delight is contemplated without any failure or wandering away to something else. The pure heart enjoys absolute concord and unity in the unshakable peace of holy spirits, the citizens of Your city in the heavens above the visible heavens.[414]

The Wise Heart

None but the wise heart is capable of the vision of God, and wisdom is the reward of the pure. Wisdom is the fullness of the knowledge of God, attained perfectly in the Beatific Vision. Wisdom, however, should not be confused with knowledge for its own sake. Rather, Augustine argues, our contemplation of truth is an essential *means* to eternal bliss, but it is not its essence. Our true quest is not for knowledge, but for *being* — to become one with God in Him. We long to know Him that we may obtain Him. Augustine writes:

> Because the highest good is known and grasped by truth, and because this truth is wisdom, let us, by our wisdom, see and grasp the highest good, and enjoy it. Happy indeed is the man who enjoys the highest good. It is this truth that reveals all true goods.[415]

Etienne Gilson clarifies Augustine's distinction between knowledge and attainment of the vision of God: "But a good is not an end if we regard it as something to be known; it is an end only in so far as it is something to be possessed. And although it is certainly true to say that knowledge of a thing means possession of a thing, we cannot say that knowledge is the same as perfect possession."[416] Perfect possession of the Beatific Vision, then, is the attainment of the wisdom of God, that is, Truth. As truth is single, the soul is happy when it is finally liberated from the torment of divided loves. Augustine rejoices in the unblemished soul's happy life: "When this very joy, born out of the attainment of this good, calmly, peacefully, and continually lifts up the spirit, it is called the happy life."[417] "O sweetest light of the purified mind! Wisdom!"[418]

The wise heart is moved by a firm faith in the veracity of God's promise of eternal joy. Indeed, Augustine avers, faith is the ground of reason. Reason apart from faith is imbecilic; reason illuminated by faith leads to wisdom. It is faith which assures the mind that God is truth, so that the faith-filled mind may lead the heart in the way of the One Truth. The way is none other than perfect obedience to His will and imitation of His love. As He is One, so the heart must be one. Augustine directs us to Holy Wisdom: "'Think of the Lord with a good heart, and in simplicity of heart seek for Him' (Ws 1:1).... Now therefore, give ear at once, and learn to long for God; learn to make ready [where you may] see God. *Blessed are the pure in heart, for they shall see God.*"[419] To see God, Augustine explains, means the soul will become a "partaker of that unchangeable Wisdom," so that it may have "'a share in the self-same,' as it is written about all the saints (see Ps 121:3).... Self-same is to be understood... as the highest and immutable good, which is God, and of His wisdom and His will, to whom it is sung in another place: 'You shall change them, and they shall be changed. But You are the same' (see Ps 101:27-28)."[420]

Participation and Continuity

The soul shall become a "partaker of that unchangeable Wisdom" in the Beatific Vision.[421] Illumination occurs by participation. Grace, that is, God's own life, is the efficient cause of beatitude. We cannot achieve the happy life of our own accord; rather, we participate in His action, in His life. Augustine explains that even the "idea of happiness is impressed upon our minds before we are happy… so, before we are wise, we have an idea of wisdom in our minds."[422] The idea of happiness is nothing other than God's own handiwork, the image of the joy of the Trinity imprinted on our nature. We are said to reflect His image interiorly insofar as we possess the capacity through grace to obtain happiness. We can say we possess God's image in accordance with the degree we possess wisdom and charity within an ordered life.[423]

At the very least, we reflect a semblance of His image insofar as humans are sentient beings who seek happiness; however, we participate in His image insofar as His grace abides in us. Now, grace is gift; we cannot command it, and neither does God compel us to receive it. We depend on God's beneficence and persevering will to bestow grace. No one knows the mind of God, but Augustine consoles us with the knowledge of our free will, which can choose to accept God's grace. The more the will unhesitatingly assents to God's gift of Himself, the freer the will becomes to choose His life, that is, grace liberates the will from the weight of concupiscence. The will, liberated from the passions, acts with purity of intention. As all goodness is derived from God, the purer we become, the fuller we participate in the purity of God's life.[424]

The goodness we derive from God is due to our adoption by Him. By His grace, we are made partakers of Himself. To be full of God is to be deified — gods, as it were. Augustine is clear we are not God according to our nature: We are human beings created by the nature of God; however, because He has removed our sin and filled us with His own life, we nonetheless partake in His divinity. The gift of participation is even sweeter, for by original sin we had descended to the farthest reaches away from heaven, but mercifully through the Son of God's participation in sinful flesh, He has lifted us to the highest life. "But when the time had fully come, God sent forth His Son, born of woman, born under the law, to redeem those who were under the law, so that we might receive adoption as sons" (Gal 4:4-5, *RSV*). Indeed, the Incarnation makes our participation a reality; He is the requirement for our heavenly reward. In a very real sense, the requirement and the reward are one, for participation in Divine Life is its own reward.[425]

> The vision is face to face (see 1 Cor 13:12), which is promised to the just as their supreme reward, and this will come to pass when [the Son] shall deliver the kingdom to God the Father. There, He wants it understood, will also be the vision of His own form, when the whole of creation together with that form in which the Son of God has been made the Son of Man, has been made subject to God. Because according to this form: 'The Son Himself will be made subject to Him, who subjected all things to Him, that God may be all in all' (see 1 Cor 15:24, 28).[426]

The *continuity* of the requirement is the participation in Christ's suffering and death. The unity of the Son of Man's *sacrifice*, from birth through death, is the means of our redemption. When we suffer in imitation of Him and for the sake of His charity, we emerge from death to life in Him. Suffering is precious gold, fashioned to brilliance in the fire of purgation. When we crucify our bodies with Christ, our hearts radiate His resurrected glory on earth, and our whole being will be radiant in the Beatific Vision, for then the "Spirit of Him who raised up Christ from the dead will dwell in you; He who raised up Christ from the dead shall enliven also your mortal bodies by His Spirit that dwells in you" (Rm 8:11).[427] Augustine assures us "the very punishment of wickedness has become the armor of virtue, and the penalty of the sinner becomes the reward of the righteous. For then death was incurred by sinning, now righteousness is fulfilled by dying."[428] The continuity of life is in the victory over death, which has been enervated through Christ. Augustine encourages his hearers with hope that springs eternal.

> We have from Him a great manifestation of great love, which belongs only to the good… [that God has] sent to us His own Word, who is His only Son, that by His birth and suffering for us in the flesh, which He assumed, we might know how much God valued man, and that by that unique sacrifice we might be purified from all our sins, and that, love being shed abroad in our hearts by His Spirit, we might, having surmounted all difficulties, come into eternal rest, and the ineffable sweetness of the contemplation of Himself.[429]

Augustine perceives a great divide between sinners and righteous. This divide exists within the heart, known to God alone, and it is as great as the divide between heaven and earth. The hearts of sinners are converted to the flesh, and so die by the flesh eternally. Their hearts are weighed down by concupiscence and are unable to rise from the filth into the light. On the other hand, the hearts cleansed by faith and tried by suffering are carried aloft by the weight of God's life in them. Their heart's *foretaste* of the fullness of God has blessed them with hope, that they may endure the distention of time patiently for the sake of obtaining His fullness, their heavenly reward. God graces them now because their hearts are pure; the eye of the heart is sound. The pure in heart live in certain hope they will be perfectly blessed in heaven, for their unspotted hearts can bear God. Augustine states: "'*Blessed are the pure in heart, for they shall see God.*' This is the end of our love; an end whereby we are perfected, and not consumed."[430] God will be our sufficiency.

BEATIFIC VISION

The Blessed: Foretaste

> Following after God is the desire of happiness; to reach
> God is happiness itself. We follow after God by loving
> Him; we reach Him, not by becoming entirely what
> He is, but in nearness to Him, and in wonderful and
> immaterial contact with Him, and in being inwardly il-
> luminated and occupied by His truth and holiness. He
> is light itself; we get enlightenment from Him.... For
> to those who love the Lord all things issue in good....
> If nothing can separate us from His love, must not this
> be surer as well as better than any other good?[431]

Augustine offers the words above to fortify our hope of the
vision of God and to console us while we endure the necessities of
living. The blessed are like Mary who sat at the feet of Jesus and
left the business of the world at bay, unlike her sister, Martha, who
occupied herself with the passing things of this world. Mary lived
as though her happy reward was in her midst and, indeed, it was.
She experienced joy because she knew in the depths of her heart
the one thing necessary for unfading happiness: the nearness of
Him. While she traversed the earth until she reached her heavenly
abode, our Lord rewarded her single hearted faith with His nearness. Through the story of Martha and Mary, Augustine affirms
that we can be blessed with a foretaste of the vision of God if our
hearts are purged of the passing things of this world.[432]

Though life is a burden to us now, when we live by faith,
hope, and love of God, our hearts and minds are set free from the
crushing weight of life's burden. Our spirits are transported to the
peace of Christ, while the flesh remains under the yoke of corruption, until God will be all in all at the resurrection of the body.
The body, however, also receives a measure of peace in this life in-

sofar as the flesh does not press upon the spirit. Where temperance and fortitude prevail, the body can be said to share in the present peace with the spirit, for the whole person — body, mind, and spirit — will be happy in heaven. Because we cannot possess the fullness of joy now, we live in hope for its attainment in the future and receive the consolation of partial joy until that happy day.[433]

Augustine asks his hearers to trust in God's providential will, for our Lord will bring to fruition the perfection begun in them when Christ comes again. Divine mercy will grant the pure in heart perseverance in the good, keeping them from sin; thus when it is time to meet their Bridegroom face to face, they shall possess the radiance required to enter into the nuptial feast. Indeed, "Christ Jesus, the Mediator between God and men, reigns now among all the just who live by faith, and shall one day bring them to that sight which [St. Paul] calls the vision 'face to face' (1 Cor 13:12)."[434]

The merit of the blessed in this life is their resemblance to Divine Charity. When they love God above all others and others for His sake, they can be said to possess the love of God which never dies. They then live by faith in the hope that they will rest eternally in His love and He in their hearts in full measure, for the desire of every heart is to love and be loved. This one truth abides, Augustine maintains, even for those who would trade love for a phantom.

> [If] any man uses this life with a reference to that other which he ardently loves and confidently hopes for, he may well be called even now blessed, though not in reality so much as in hope. But the actual possession of the happiness of this life, without the hope of what is beyond, is but a false happiness and profound misery. For the true blessings of the soul are not now enjoyed; for that is not true wisdom which does not direct all its prudent observations, manly actions, virtuous self-

restraint, and just arrangements, to that end which God shall be all in all in a secure eternity and perfect peace.[435]

In the present, the pure in heart enjoy the peace of the contemplation of God through faith. Faith is His gift to us; by grace it is the cause and consequence of a clean heart, whose purity alone allows for ascent to the heights of contemplation. The very act of purgation moves the heart to cleave to God, the intellect to comprehend Him, and the eye to behold Him partially — but ever so clearly — until heart and mind so resemble the love and wisdom of God that the eye is brought to full sight in the Beatific Vision. Then, Augustine proclaims, the soul will have attained the perfect peace of God. God will be seen *face to face*. The pure in heart will be filled with the fullness of God. Indeed, we do not fill God; rather we are *full* of God, the Holy Trinity. "'Follow peace with all men, and holiness, without which no man shall see God' (Heb 12:14). For by this is the heart purified; for in it is that faith 'which works by love.' Hence, *'Blessed are the pure in heart, for they shall see God.'*"[436] The vision of God's comeliness, Augustine reiterates, is "to the godly alone. On account of their love for Him does He promise this very thing, that He will show Himself to them."[437]

Augustine is aware that many souls who had striven towards purity of heart in this life had died before they were able to attain the perfection which avails for heaven. He counsels the living to take heart, for God's mercy has afforded these souls the gift of temporal, purgative punishment beyond this life. The words of Scripture, upheld by our Catholic faith, offer this blessed assurance: "Who can endure the day of [the Lord's] coming, and who can stand when He appears? For He is like a refiner's fire and like fullers' soap; He will sit as a refiner and purify the descendants of Levi and refine them like gold and silver, until they present offerings to the Lord in righteousness" (Ml 3:2-3, *RSV*).[438]

The refiner's fire is a purgatorial punishment; whereby, after death the soul which is not so disfigured by sin that it merits eternal damnation will undergo the final rinse, more or less according to the soul's condition. Indeed, only the pure heart is capable of receiving Pure Love. "On that day the branch of the Lord shall be beautiful and glorious... once the Lord has washed away the filth of the daughters of Zion and cleansed the bloodstains of Jerusalem from its midst by a spirit of judgment and by a spirit of burning" (Is 4:4, *RSV*). Augustine adds that God answers the prayers of the Church for these souls with mercy; their punishment will cease, and they will enter their heavenly reward.[439]

The Beatified: Face to Face

> Finally, when the heart shall cleave to Him completely, it will be one spirit, and the Apostle bears witness to this when he says: 'But he who cleaves to the Lord is one spirit' (see 1 Cor 6:17) by drawing near, of course, in order to partake of that nature, truth, and blessedness, but yet without any increase in Him or His nature, truth, and blessedness. In that nature, therefore, to which the mind will blissfully adhere, it will live unchangeably, and all that it sees, it will see as unchangeable. Then, as the divine Scripture promises, its desires will be satisfied with good things (see Ps 102:5), with unchangeable goods, with the Trinity itself, its God, whose image it is; and that nothing may ever henceforth injure it, it will be in the secret of His face (see Ps 30:21), so filled with His abundance that it will never find delight in committing sin.[440]

In an instant we are changed from death to life and so from inconstancy to constancy, from multiplicity to simplicity, from anxiety to peace, from chaos to perfect order, from tribulation to joy, from promise to fulfillment, from knowledge to wisdom. Augustine sums up the transfiguration of the soul in the Beatific Vision as its deification: "'When He appears, we shall be like Him, for we shall see Him as He is' (1 Jn 3:2). 'As He is' Lord will be ours to see."[441] Our whole being will be illuminated, so His luminescence will be visible to the eyes of the heart. The mind, too, will know Him purely with the wisdom of His holy angels; however, unlike the angels who are pure spirit, at the resurrection of the body, we will be the perfect unity of body and soul, the perfect unity of Divine Life transfiguring the creature.[442]

We will behold the vision of God with our whole being, not just the eye of the heart, for He will fill our entirety, and we will make our abode in Him. All faculties of the transfigured shall be used to see God, for what else is the Beatific Vision but the perfect unity of being resting in the contemplation of God, seeing Him in ourselves, in one another, and in all, *in Him*. The whole heavenly chorus will praise God as one body, yet there will remain the individuality of being. There will exist a mutuality of understanding and knowledge among the saints; each will know the thoughts of the other, for there are no shadows of being in heaven. Augustine effuses: "How great shall be that felicity, which shall be tainted with no evil, which shall lack no good, and which shall afford leisure for the praises of God, who shall be all in all!... 'Blessed are they who dwell in Thy house, O Lord; they will be still praising' (Ps 84:4)."[443]

The saints enjoy the perfection of virtue, and the absence of vice insures imperviousness to corruption, thus immortality. Whereas those who suffer the punishment for evil endure an endless death, the saints enjoy everlasting life. There is a true distinction here between immortality and endless death, as the wicked experience the unending agony of corruption, while the saints in light reap the fullness of life. The former are tormented by the unfulfilled desire of want; the latter rejoice in the satisfaction of plenty. God is the satisfaction of the saints. Augustine explains this is what St. Paul means when he says: "'That God may be all in all' (1 Cor 15:28). He shall be the end of our desires who shall be seen without end, loved without cloy, praised without weariness."[444]

Augustine distinguishes the nature of the will before the Fall and the will in eternal bliss. The will that is redeemed shall enjoy even greater freedom than the liberty enjoyed by our first parents because of God's superabundant grace bestowed on sinners. The saints in light partake in His impeccability. Their will shall recall sin but not be lured by it, and the saved shall also keep in mind the damned. This recollection and knowledge will not disturb their peace and tranquility, but serve only as the impetus to sing the praises of God's mercy, for the blessed in heaven have been freed from the inclination to sin altogether.

> The first freedom of will which man received when he was created upright consisted in an ability not to sin, but also in an ability to sin; whereas this last freedom of will shall be superior, inasmuch as it shall not be able to sin. This, indeed, shall not be a natural ability, but the gift of God. God by nature cannot sin, but the partaker of God receives this inability from God…. the former [will] being adapted to the acquiring of merit, the latter to the enjoying of the reward…. [In the city of God] there shall be free will, one in all the citizens, and indivisible in each, delivered from all ill, filled with all good, enjoying indefeasibly the delights of eternal joys, oblivious of sins, oblivious of sufferings, and yet not so oblivious as to be ungrateful to its Deliverer.[445]

The Church shall convey these spotless souls to the Beatific Vision, and the Church, herself, will be the heavenly form of the Body. Those who live and die sanctified in Mother Church shall be borne aloft to rest in her *within Him*. At the end of the world, when the angels arrive to separate the wicked from the righteous, those found in the bosom of Mother Church, truly cleaving to her as to the Lord's net cast into the sea, will be brought together into Him. He will say to those whom He gathers: "Come, receive the kingdom." These are those who lived by faith in Him and in hope for all His promises, who died with Him in Baptism, conformed to His virtue in life, and remained with Him under the precepts of His Church and her Scriptures.[446] When they enter their heavenly abode, Augustine writes, "sight shall displace faith; and hope shall be swallowed up in that perfect bliss to which we shall come; love, on the other hand, shall wax greater when all these fail."[447]

We will dwell in the charity of the Holy Trinity and know God as He is, but we will not see the very *essence* of Him, for only He is "Being in essence," that is, "everything which He possesses."[448] As partakers of Him, we are not Him but creatures limited according to God's design. We will not feel any lack of knowledge, however, for we will be wise in truth, the truth that to be in Him is happiness. We will be filled to capacity, so that the fullness of His charity will engender no jealousy or pride. Augustine praises the Trinity's beneficence in a meditation on the Lord's prayer: "'Glory to God in the highest,' and on earth peace to men of goodwill' (Lk 2:14), so that when our goodwill has gone before, which follows Him who has called us, the will of God is perfected in us as it is in the heavenly angels; so that no antagonism stands in the way of our blessedness: and this is peace."[449]

Augustine stresses the intimacy of the person with God in his discussion of the distribution of heavenly gifts according to God's will and in proportion to the heart's gratitude in life. There are ranks of joy in the heavenly realm, but because one shall receive joy according to one's fullness, everyone will be happy for the other. As among the angels, there are the greater ones, such as the seraphim, so among the beatified there will be those known as the great saints, and the heavenly host rejoices all the more for their presence. Augustine preaches on the glory of the saints: "After the winnowing of the Day of Judgment, the multitude of saints will appear resplendent by the reason of their glory, powerful by their merits, and manifesting the mercy of their Redeemer."[450]

Augustine is confident the saint will rise as the whole person, body and soul; the body will be resurrected and join the soul. The body will be transfigured as a spiritual body, such that the imperfections of the physical body will be gone. "There will be a harmony of the body in heaven."[451] Augustine opines each body will maintain its singular identity according to the likeness of the former self, but all parts will be brought together according to the prime of life; thus the youngest to the oldest will attain fullness of body and spirit. Augustine maintains a differentiation according to gender, as the complementarity of persons created in the image of the Blessed Trinity will remain. There will, however, be no marriage, for the bodies will not be subject to sexual intercourse or to procreation. God will complete what was lacking in life. Where there were limbs missing, there will be fullness. Should the body have been burned or scattered, God will gather all the particles from the earth and bring them together into a perfect whole. Even the unborn children will be brought to their prime. Augustine trusts in the Lord's compassion to bring completion of body to the babe in the womb no matter at what stage of development the child was lost through abortion or miscarriage.[452]

The transfigured body will be composed of perfect beauty and proportion; however, unsurpassed beauty will fall to those who bear the visible marks of the martyrs' wounds, in union with the wounds of Christ — present for all eternity as testament to the unfathomable measure of His love. These wounds are a participation in Christ's suffering for the sake of the salvation of souls, and they are cause for great rejoicing among the heavenly hosts. Augustine speaks of this mark of honor:

> But the love we bear to the blessed martyrs causes us,
> I know not how, to desire to see in the heavenly king-

dom the marks of the wounds which they received for the name of Christ, and possibly we shall see them. For this will not be a deformity, but a mark of honor, and will add luster to their appearance, and a spiritual, if not a bodily beauty. And yet we need not believe that they to whom it has been said, "Not a hair of your head shall perish," shall, in the resurrection, want such of their members as they have been deprived of in their martyrdom. But if it will be seemly in that new kingdom to have some marks of these wounds still visible in that immortal flesh, the places where they have been wounded or mutilated shall retain the scars without any of the members being lost. While, therefore, it is quite true that no blemishes which the body has sustained shall appear in the resurrection, yet we are not to reckon or name these marks of virtue blemishes.[453]

"Blessed are the pure in heart, for they shall see God." Augustine writes in order that we may know the path to the Beatific Vision is by way of godliness. The heart that bears our Lord's image of purity in all things undergoes a true transformation; whereby, even as we sojourn, the heart holds His grace and beholds His glory, truly but incompletely. When this life passes into the next, those of us who have attained purity of heart will see Him face to face, and because of His unbounded charity, we will see ourselves also in His countenance, for He has taken us into Himself, there to dwell forever and ever.

Conclusion

Blessed are the pure in heart, for they shall see God.

For Augustine, the meaning of these words of Christ is clear: The relationship between purity of heart and the vision of God is organic, such that those who defile their own hearts through selfish attachments are intrinsically unable to behold the God who is perfect love. Positively stated: Those who purify their hearts through single-minded love of God, with the assistance of grace, so transfigure their hearts as to become sharers in the divine life, partially in the world and fully in heaven. This is the way of perfection towards participation in the Beatific Vision, initiated by the Incarnation of the Son of God and obtained in steps through faith in Him, an upright will, exemplary virtue, suffering, prayer, and good works.

We began with an investigation into the ways in which key experiences in Augustine's life influenced his conversion to the Catholic Church and his development of doctrine. This brief biographical examination followed Augustine's lead, the writing of his *Confessions*; whereby, he delved into the events of his own life from the backward gaze of faith to understand their impact on his heart, will, and intellect, with the forward purpose of leading others to the same faith. Augustine was able to discern the constant thread that runs through a life: the quest for happiness, that is, to love and be loved. For many years, Augustine relied on the natural gifts of his intellect to satisfy his heart's desire. He found, however, that the love he sought eluded him. Eventually, he was brought to the light of faith by the grace of God, which was imparted to Him through the divine Word of Scripture, the preaching and teaching of mentors and friends, and the suffering love and patient prayers of his mother.

Happiness, Augustine discovered, resides in truth and is arrived at in the body of Christ, specifically His Church. Within the Church is order and wholeness; thus he realized the happiness he previously sought through the satisfaction of disordered desires resembled nothing of true happiness. Heart was both the cause of his disorder and its cure. Heart is at the center of Augustine's *Confessions*; heart is formed and governed by a like-minded will. Throughout his life, he detected a movement of heart and will *from* captivity to concupiscence *to* the freedom and harmony of a purified heart and will cleaving to the constancy of charity. He was awestruck by his own changed heart's capacity to know and love God with the *same* love of His Son. Through scriptural study, he discerned that the transformation of heart from corruption to incorruption is the God-ordained requisite for the Beatific Vision. In fact, the heart becomes intrinsically capable of receiving this gift precisely because it has changed.

The argument for the organic relationship between the requirement and the reward stands or falls depending on the understanding of the effect of original sin on human nature. Here, we distinguished between Christianity's two most prevalent and sharply divided conceptualizations of post-lapsarian human nature: the Catholic and Reformation understandings paradigmatically expressed in the writings of Augustine and Luther. The point was not to present an exhaustive study of nature, especially considering the divergences in Protestant thought which have developed over the centuries. Rather, it was to demonstrate that an unbreachable divide exists between Catholic and Reformation theology in their basic tenets.

The Reformation view of forensic justification requires the imputation of the righteousness of Christ, which is necessarily alien to a thoroughly corrupt nature. Freedom of the will to assent to the movement of grace is thereby precluded. Grace *imposes* purity on the decrepit heart; thus there can be no organic growth in sanctity. God "cleanses" the heart extrinsically by the action of His grace apart from the bound will. The heart and will do not change; thus the positive effects of God's grace, notably contrition and the acquisition of virtue, are not efficacious towards the attainment of the Beatific Vision. The heart, itself, remains forever unworthy of the vision of God because the imposition of grace does not effect a transformation. At the resurrection of the dead, the redeemed do not rise with transfigured hearts but with Christ *covering* their fallen natures, such that their contemplation is limited to seeing Christ *over* themselves and others.

Augustine expresses the Catholic belief in the resurrection of the body; whereby, the individual's body and soul are transfigured to contemplate the Trinity and the company of saints as they are in God. This elevated view of the person is rooted in the understanding of nature as inherently good, albeit severely weakened by the Fall. The goodness of nature extends to its will; whereby, a semblance of freedom remains. Augustine maintains the essential need for grace in the justification of the sinner and the transformation of nature; however, he also holds that grace works towards the preservation of freedom. Within God's inscrutable wisdom, the will is more fully free insofar as grace moves it. The free action of the will to conform to the will of God effects a cleansing of the heart that is true, lasting, and habitual. For one to attain the Beatific Vision, the heart must bear the vision of God within itself. *"Blessed are the pure in heart for they shall see God."* The relationship between the requirement and the reward is thus organic.

The will, moved and assisted by grace, is responsible for the heart's transformation, for it is the will conforming to God's will, which inclines the faculties to renounce sin and conform to the good. As the movement of the will stretches upwards towards the loftiness of God, the whole person is cleansed of sin and its impure effects. An extended treatment of original sin, grace, and holiness provided a deeper understanding of the condition of the post-lapsarian will and its influences on the heart's affections. The Pelagian heresy compelled Augustine to develop a comprehensive doctrine of grace, in which he maintains the integrity of grace's efficaciousness and the freedom of the will. By the grace of God the will is free, and it is graced all the more as it acts in freedom for the good.

The will inclined towards the good moves the heart to cleave to the Supreme Good, the Holy Trinity. When Augustine speaks of heart, he is speaking of the inner person. The heart is natural because we are created beings; however, the fulfillment of human nature is to partake in Divine Nature. This participation is a gift from God's mercy and love, made manifest through the Incarnation, passion and death of Christ. While the heart will never become divine essence, the heart can possess divine love, which so transforms the heart that it is deified; that is, our human nature is transfigured by its unity with God and fullness of Him. This is the Beatific Vision; whereby, the heart rests in perfect contemplation within the perfect charity of the Blessed Trinity.

The heart, as the center of one's being, is integrally related to all the faculties, such that they conform to the heart's desires for good or for ill. Indeed, the faculties will be one in the One God when He is all in all. The heart that wills only the Good will reap the Beatific Vision. Faith is the ground and sustenance of the heart's hope. Faith in Christ compels the heart to conform to the way of the cross; whereby, the heart loves God singly with an utterly self-emptying love. By this love, the heart crucifies the passions of the flesh for Christ's sake and imitates the virtue of Christ in love of neighbor for His sake. This is the way of perfection: The heart undergoes a daily cleansing in the humility of

Christ and so grows in the fullness of the image of God, which is sublime simplicity.

The pure in heart have embraced spiritual virginity, for Christ, the Bridegroom, will take only the spotless bride unto Himself. Whereas sin came into the world through concupiscence, so salvation — the Savior — came through detached love, the love of Mary, the mother of Christ, and the Church, His body. The offspring of spiritual continence is purity of heart which is fulfilled in the happy estate of life everlasting. Those who are continent in body and spirit have chosen the better part. They are living foretastes of the heavenly joy, and they share most intimately in the fecundity of Mary and the Church.

We cleanse the heart by faith in God within the bosom of His Church. There, the sacraments are administered, especially Baptism and the Eucharist, in which we are washed clean by the power of His Spirit and "touch" Him in the reception of His Body and His Blood. Prayer, fasting, and almsgiving are invaluable means of cleansing the heart, after the example and instruction of our Lord when He taught us to pray.

God counts the pristine souls as blessed on earth. He imparts to them His gift of Divine Life, grace, so that the pure in heart begin to live the Beatific Vision in the here and now, possessing the wisdom of God truly, albeit incompletely. The change in the heart is organic, such that the heart is transfigured. It becomes the partaker of Divine Life as it is being cleansed. The constancy of Divine Providence assures us that the good work begun in this life will continue in the next, where the pure in heart will be transfigured wholly, body and soul. The whole person will see God face to face and rest eternally in His countenance.

ENDNOTES

¹ *Confessions* 1.1.1 (Chadwick).

² See *On the Grace of Christ, and On Original Sin*, 1.7.7ff., in *Nicene and Post Nicene Fathers* I, vol. 5. See Peter J. Riga, "Created Grace in St. Augustine," *Augustinian Studies* 3 (1972), p. 115; *Free Choice of the Will*, 3.7.70ff., trans. Anna S. Benjamin and L. H. Hackstaff (Indianapolis: The Bobbs-Merrill Co., Inc., 1964); Ibid. See *Epistle* 171A, CSEL 44:632-36. See also Agostino Trape, "Saint Augustine" in *Patrology*, volume 4, edited by Angelo Di Berardino, introduction by Angelo Quasten and translated by Placid Solari (Westminster, MD: Christian Classics, 1986), p. 454: "The essential points of Augustine's spiritual doctrine can be summarized under the following headings: the universal vocation to holiness; charity as the center, soul and measure of Christian perfection; humility as the indispensable condition for the development of charity; purification as the law of interior ascent; prayer as a duty and a necessity, the means and the end of spiritual life; and the degrees of the spiritual life."

³ *Our Lord's Sermon on the Mount* 1.4.12.

⁴ *Sermon* 261.4 (FC, vol. 38).

⁵ See *Epistle* 171.

⁶ *Confessions* 10.27.38 (Chadwick).

⁷ See Benjamin and Hackstaff, *Free Choice of the Will*, Introduction, pp. xv ff.

⁸ See *On Christian Doctrine* 2.7.12ff.; 3.1.2ff.; 2.14.21ff; 2.11.16; 2.31.48 for extensive explanations of the primacy of Scripture and its various usages.

⁹ See *Sermon* 240.3. See also *Free Choice of the Will*, Introduction by Benjamin and Hackstaff, pp. xx ff.; Chadwick, *Confessions*, Introduction, p. xxiii: "From the first paragraph of the *Confessions* onwards, Augustine can express Neoplatonic themes in language which sounds like a pastiche of the Psalter. It is among the paradoxes of the work that the author wholly rejected pagan religious cult, but accepted a substantial proportion of Neoplatonic theology, so that the reader is surprised to discover how constantly echoes of Plotinus occur. A famous passage in book VII [of his *Confessions*] finds the essentials of Platonism in the prologue to St. John's Gospel, yet with the crucial exception of the incarnation. 'That the Word was made flesh I did not read there (in the books of the Platonists).' At the end of the same book he observes that those books had nothing to say about penitential confession or the Eucharistic thanksgiving for our redemption. Yet when he describes the vision at Ostia shared by Monica and himself (perhaps a unique instance of a mystical experience for two simultaneously) the vocabulary is deeply indebted to Plotinus."

¹⁰ See Peter Brown, *Augustine of Hippo* (Berkeley: University of California Press, 1967); Henry Chadwick, *Augustine* (New York: Oxford University Press, 1986); *Augustine* (Jacques Maritain Center: www.nd.edu/Departments/Maritain/etext/augustin.htm.). See also Mary T. Clark, *Augustine: Philosopher of Freedom* (New York: Desclee, 1958). Clark writes about Platonic philosophy: "Responsibility as a fact universally accepted is recognized, but it is not really made intelligible. Free-

dom from ignorance seems to be the only requirement for virtue. Even the Platonic *Eros*, the universal tendency of all things towards the Good (Plato *Republic*, VI, 505-506) is an intellectual thirst, a craving to participate in the Supreme Intelligible — the Idea of the Good. So-called Platonic love is predominantly the need for fulfillment rather than the free gift of a personal preference for the beloved.... The moral intellectualism that is the Platonic ethic has not given to an individuality its proper value because Plato lacked the notion of the person, which alone guarantees true notions of responsibility and of human love — responsibility through autonomous free choice and human love through an objective love for the good."

11   See Chadwick, *Augustine*. See also Etienne Gilson, *The Christian Philosophy of St. Augustine* (New York, Random House, 1960), Introduction.

12   Mark Vessey, "*Opus Imperfectum*: Augustine and His Readers, A.D. 426-35."

13   See Ibid., p. 6; *Confessions* 7.5.8 (Chadwick): "Since we were too weak to discover the truth by pure reasoning and therefore needed the authority of the sacred writings, I now began to believe that You would never have conferred such preeminent authority on the Scripture, now diffused through all lands, unless You had willed that it would be a means of coming to faith in You and a means of seeking to know You."

14   *City of God* 18.51, trans. by Marcus Dods (New York: The Modern Library, Random House, Inc., 1950).

15   *Reply to Faustus the Manichean* 11.4f. See Vessey, p. 6; Trape, p. 445ff. See also Glenn Tinder, "Augustine's World and Ours" in *First Things* (December, 1997), no. 78, p. 35ff.

16   See *Letters* 28.3.3; 82.1.3; 137.1.3; *Against Faustus the Manichaean* 11.5.

17   *Against Faustus the Manichaean* 28.2; *Against Julian* 6.5.11; *On Christian Doctrine* 2.8f; *On Baptism* 3.2.2. See *Of the Morals of the Catholic Church* 29.29.59, on the ill use of Scripture by the Manicheans. See also *Reply to Faustus the Manichean* 32 and 33 for Augustine's painstaking reply to Manichean ill-use of Scripture and his correction.

18   See *City of God* 22:30: "We must first show how Jesus Christ speaks in the prophetical books under the title of the Lord God, while yet there can be no doubt that it is Jesus Christ who speaks; so that in other passages where this is not at once apparent, and where nevertheless it is said that the Lord God will come to that last judgment, we may understand that Jesus Christ is meant." See also *Sermons on New Testament Lessons*, 77.1-4; *Homilies on the Gospel of John*, 9.2.1ff.

19   *On Christian Doctrine* 2.10f.; *City of God* 15-17. See Peter Brown, *Augustine of Hippo*, p. 255; See also *On Christian Doctrine* 1.1ff; 3.12f; 4.27f., on the uses of Scripture; Boniface Ramsey, *Beginning to Read the Fathers* (Mahwah, New Jersey: Paulist Press, 1985), chapter 2.

20   *Expositions on the Psalms* 3.1 (NPNF I, vol. 8).

21   See *On the Trinity* 1.1.2; *City of God* 2.21f.; *On Christian Doctrine* 2.7f. Augustine employs the tools of allegory and typology especially in his Old Testament exegesis to demonstrate the Hebrew narratives are revelations of Christ. He argues that the faithful must study Scripture in this way because our knowledge has gone from direct to indirect since the Fall. We now see partially, aided by signs, symbols, allegories, and types. See also *On the Catholic and Manichaean Ways of Life*, 16.26ff; Boniface Ramsey, chapters 2f; Thomas Finan and Vincent Twomey, *Scriptural Interpretation in the Fathers: Letter and Spirit* (Dublin: Four Courts Press, 1995).

22   *On the Trinity* 14.9.12.

23   *On Christian Doctrine* 2.40 (NPNF I, vol. 2).

24   See *City of God* 10.23. See also Jaroslav Pelikan, *The Mystery of Continuity: Time and History, Memory and Eternity in the Thought of Saint Augustine* (Charlottesville: University of Virginia) p. 55; Bruno Switalski, *Neoplatonism and the Ethics of St. Augustine* (New York: Polish Institute of Arts and Sciences in America, 1946).

25   See *Confessions* 53.3; *On Christian Doctrine* 2.40; Trape, p. 405. For a discussion on Augustine's use of language and the effect of the reader, see Brian Stock, *Augustine the Reader* (Cambridge, MA: The Belknap Press of Harvard University Press, 1996): "[Stock's] aim is to analyze Augustine's own various statements about reading within the evolution of his ideas and to describe his responses to specific occasions, audiences, and controversies.... The notion of the self-conscious reader plays an important part in his resolution of key issues in the philosophy of mind," pp. 3ff.

26   *City of God* 77.3f.

27   *Confessions* 8.1.1 (Chadwick).

28   *Epistle* 171A, CSEL 44:632-36. See *Confessions* 9.6.14; 9.10.23; 11.29.39; *On the Trinity* 8.4.6.

29   *On the Grace of Christ, and On Original Sin* 1.7.7ff; 1.15.14. See Henry Chadwick, *Augustine* (New York: Oxford, 1986), p. 107.

30   *Sermon on the Mount* 2.7.43; *Expositions on the Psalms* 4.9. See *Free Choice of the Will* 3.7.69ff; Introduction, pp. xxv-xvi. See also Gertrude Gillette, "Purity of Heart in St. Augustine" in *Purity of Heart in Early Ascetic and Monastic Literature* (Collegeville, MN: Liturgical Press, 1999), pp. 178ff.

31   Ibid., 3.7.70ff. See *Tractates on the Gospel of John* 8.4. See also Clark, pp. 3, 133 on the freedom of the will to respond in kind. Clark writes: "Without God life is meaningless and very confusing. Life is meant to be a dialogue between the love of God and the love of man. In this dialogue God is the first speaker, and man's free will is his faculty of response to God. Through free will, man's whole being can respond. Because such response is possible, man is responsible for what he says to God and for what he does not say. This is the dialogue that brings God into time and man into eternity. Only right-ordered love can bring this successfully to pass, and that is why the love of God is the chief commandment."

32   *Our Lord's Sermon on the Mount* 2.5.18 (ACW, vol. 5).

33   *Epistle* 171A, CSEL 44:632-36. The headings are not in the original.

34   *Sermon* 261.4 (FC, vol. 38): "Do you really wish to see? Do you desire to see something good, something great? I urge you: wish for it.... 'Blessed are the clean of heart, for they shall see God' (Mt 5:8). First, then, think about purifying your heart; consider this an obligation; enlist all your energies for this task; be intent upon this work. What you desire to see is clean; the place from which you wish to see is unclean." See *Sermon* 261.7 (FC, vol. 38): "Cleanse your heart, so far as you can. Work at this; accomplish this. Ask, beg, and humble yourself so that God may cleanse the place where He is to abide." See also Etienne Gilson, *The Christian Philosophy of St. Augustine* (New York: Random House, 1960).

35   See the *Canons of the Council of Orange* (529 A.D.) on the *Internet Christian Library* (www.iclnet.org/pub/resources/text/history/council.orange.txt) for a wider discussion of the effects of original sin and grace on the human race.

36   This study employs Luther as the paradigm for the thought of the Protestant
     Reformers; however, it is acknowledged that the Reformers do not speak for all
     Protestantism, especially those associated with the English Reformation and later
     developments in certain Protestant sects. Since Vatican II, especially, there has been
     a concerted effort on the part of Roman Catholics and Protestants to discover ar-
     eas of consensus in thought and belief. One document which makes great strides
     towards this end is the *Lutheran-Catholic Declaration on the Doctrine of Justification*
     (1998), which can be found at www.elca/org/ecumenical/ecumenicaldialogue/ro-
     mancatholic/jddj/declaration.html.

37   Ernst Kasemann, *Commentary on Romans* (Grand Rapids, MI: William B. Eerd-
     mans Publishing Co., 1980), p. 185. While there is a body of research on the sub-
     ject of the possibility of perfection in Luther's writings, their argument does not
     cancel out the *simul* nature of the human being, which is pertinent to this pres-
     ent discussion. See Karl Herman Schelkle, *The Epistle to the Romans* (New York:
     Herder and Herder, 1964) p. 103; Hans Conzelmann, *1 Corinthians* (Philadelphia:
     Fortress Press, 1975), p. 21; C. K. Barrett, *The First Epistle to the Corinthians* (New
     York: Harper and Row Publishers, 1968) p. 60, 142f.

38   *Sermon* 184.1 (FC, vol. 38). See *On the Trinity* 4.14.19; 13.14.18.

39   *Admonition and Grace* 12:35. See Ibid., 12.38 (FC, vol. 2): "God effects in them
     the will itself. The result is that, since there is no perseverance without the power
     and the will to persevere, both the possibility and the will to persevere are given
     them by the bounty of divine grace. Their will is so roused by the Holy Spirit that
     they are able to persevere, because they will to do so; and they will to do so, because
     God effects this will, and consequently, whatever its weakness, it does not fail, and
     is not overcome by any difficulty.... An aid was given to the weakness of the hu-
     man will, with the result that it is unwaveringly and invincibly influenced by divine
     grace."

40   See Pelikan on the Augustinian view of nature, p. 74: "Corrupted but not completely
     destroyed by the fall into sin, this image of God was the guarantee of the continuity
     between the state of nature and the state of grace. Because it was conferred as the
     image of God the Creator, this continuity of human nature would perpetuate itself
     even in spite of human sin." See Frederick H. Russell, "Only Something Good Can
     Be Evil: The Genesis of Augustine's Secular Ambivalence," *Theological Studies* 51
     (December 1, 1990), pp. 298ff.

41   *Free Choice of the Will* 1.12.85-87. See Clark, p. 3: "There have been attempts by
     critics to bring Augustine's statements concerning free will and concerning free-
     dom into contradiction. Yet in Augustine's own experience, when that experience is
     viewed in its full theological dimensions, the realities of free choice and of freedom
     are reconciled. He learned that for the slavery of doing evil the human will sufficed,
     but for the freedom of doing good both man's consent and God's grace are needed.
     Augustine's defense of free will as a reality and as a source of responsibility is more
     than a polemical answer to Manicheans — it is a recall to the sense of sin…. [It is]
     more than a polemical answer to the Pelagians — recall to the sense of the dignity
     of man and of the greatness of God."

42   *Sermon* 212.1; *On the Gift of Perseverance* 13.33.

43   *On the Trinity* 13.10.14; *Confessions* 7.16.22; 8.9.21f.; *Expositions on the Psalms*
     99.8-10. See *Against Two Letters of the Pelagians* 1.37; *On Nature and Grace* 14.45;
     Sermons 27.4; *Letters* 120.3.13. See also Stephen Pfurtner, *Luther and Aquinas on
     Salvation* (New York: Sheed and Ward, 1964), pp. 29ff.; Trape, pp. 427, 440.

44 *On the Gospel of St. John* 101.16.5.

45 Luther, *Smalcald Article* 292.

46 Luther, *Apology* 131, 116-119; *Proceedings at Augsburg, 1518*, LW 31:270-29; *Lectures on Romans*, 1516, LW 25:71 and LW 25:104; *Formula of Concord*, 524; *Ten Sermons on the Catechism*, 1528, LW 51:166.

47 Luther, *Apology* 123f. See Ibid., 112, 152-54, ref. Rm 4:5 and 120, ref. Rm 10:10; *Lectures on Galatians* 1535, LW 26:8; *Invocovit Sermon* 1522, LW 51:70; *Luther's Prayers* 17-18; *Lecture on Hebrews* 1516; *Formula of Concord* 428, 424, ref. Rm 3:8; 543: "The only essential and necessary elements of justification are the grace of God, the merit of Christ, and faith, which accepts these in the promise of the Gospel, whereby the righteousness of Christ is reckoned to us and by which we obtain the forgiveness of sin, reconciliation with God, adoption, and the inheritance of eternal life."

48 Luther, *Luther's Prayers* 607.

49 Luther, *Formula of Concord* 424, 539, 542f., 565.

50 Luther, *Lectures on Romans*, LW 25:68, 74.

51 Luther, *Formula of Concord* 544.

52 Luther, *The Freedom of a Christian*, 1520, LW 31:351. See *Letter to George Spalatin*, 1516, LW 48:13.

53 Luther, *Lectures on Romans*, 1516, LW 25:26.

54 Ibid. See Luther, *Fourteen Consolations*, 1520, LW 42:140ff.

55 Luther, *Fourteen Consolations*, 1520, LW 42:140-42. See Joseph A. Burgess, "Rewards, But in a Very Different Sense" in *Lutheran-Roman Catholic Dialogue, 1985*. See also Augustine *contra* Luther in *Free Choice of the Will* 2.1.7: "Both punishment and reward would be unjust if man did not have free will. Moreover, there must needs be justice both in punishment and in reward, since justice is one of the goods that are from God."

56 *Letter* 152.2.10 in Trape, p. 440. See Ibid.: "'He who created you without your cooperation does not justify you without your wanting it.' (*Serm.* 11.13). The proof can be reduced to the Christological motive that Christ, according to Scripture, is judge and savior: 'If grace does not exist, how does He save the world? If there is no free will, how does He judge the world?'" (*Letter* 214.2); See also *On Forgiveness of Sins, and Baptism* 2.33.17 on the healing of the will through efficient grace and the strengthening of the will through assisting grace.

57 *On Forgiveness of Sins, and Baptism* 2.23.21. See Ibid., 2.27.17 on the single-minded obedience of Christ; 2.33.17 on the single-minded obedience of the will through the grace of Christ.

58 *Confessions* 11.29.39 (Chadwick). See *On the Gospel of John* 105.17.2ff; *On Man's Perfection in Righteousness* 19.40 (NPNF I, vol. 5).

59 Ibid., 2.1.1 (Chadwick).

60 Ibid., 8.5.10.

61 See *Confessions* 1.20.31; 2.2.2.

62 *Confessions* 2.6.14. See Peter Brown, *Augustine of Hippo*, p. 244.

63 Ibid., 9.1.1. (Chadwick).

64 Brown, *Augustine of Hippo*, p. 246.

65   *Confessions* 2.3.8 (Chadwick). See Ibid., 2.3.7.

66   Brown, p. 250. See pp. 154, 224.

67   *Confessions*, 2.3.8 (Chadwick).

68   Ibid., 2.9.17 (Chadwick).

69   Ibid., 2.10.18. See 10.36.59 (Chadwick).

70   Brown, *Augustine of Hippo*, p. 261. See *Letter* 214.2.

71   See Ibid., p. 366. See also Gerald Bonner, *Augustine and Modern Research on Pelagianism* (Philadelphia: Villanova University Press, 1972), p. 16.

72   *Confessions* 11.29 (Chadwick), *emphases* added.

73   Ibid., 7.26.22 (Chadwick). See *City of God* 13.20 (Dods), on the transgression of "pure and simple obedience" in the Fall.

74   See *Confessions* 1.7.11; 1.20.31; *Free Choice of the Will* 2.17.179. *Faith, Hope, and Charity* 3.9; 8.23; 8.27; *City of God* 11.18; 12.3; 12.22 (Dods); Bonner, p. 43.

75   *Confessions* 2.2.4 (Chadwick): "You fashion pain to be a lesson (LXX Ps. 3:20), you 'strike to heal,' you bring death upon us so that we should not die apart from you.' (Dt 32:39)." See *Confessions* 2.6.14; 3.8.16.

76   *City of God* 14.13. See Ibid., 14.15 (Dods).

77   Ibid., 14.3 (Dods).

78   *Free Choice of the Will* 2.1.5. See Ibid., 2.7; *Confessions* 5.7.13; 2.7.15. See also William Lane Craig, "Augustine on Foreknowledge and Free Will" in *Augustinian Studies* 15 (1984), p. 52.

79   *Confessions* 3.8.16. See *City of God* 13.1; 13.4; 14.14; *Faith, Hope, and Charity* 4.13; 8.25f.; 13.45; *On the Grace of Christ, and On Original Sin* 20. See also Pelikan, pp. 74f.; Stephen McKenna, trans. *The Trinity* (Washington, DC: Catholic University, 1963), p. 13; Bonner, p. 17; John D. Godsey, "The Interpretation of Romans in the History of the Christian Faith" in *Interpretation* (January, 1980), p. 8.

80   *City of God* 14.14. See *Faith, Hope, and Charity* 13.45.

81   *On the Grace of Christ, and On Original Sin*, 22 (NPNF I, vol. 5).

82   *Confessions* 1.6.7. See Ibid., 2.1.1; 2.10.18; 3.2.4; 5.7.13; 7.12.18; *City of God* 1.15; Pelikan, pp. 74f..

83   Ibid., 10.3.4 (Chadwick).

84   Ibid., 2.6.13f.

85   Ibid., 2.8.16; 2.9.17.

86   Ibid., 2.3.9 (Chadwick). See Ibid., 2.6.14.

87   Ibid., 1.7.11-12; 10,3.5.

88   Ibid., 2.2.2 (Chadwick).

89   *On the Trinity* p. 13 (FC, vol. 45)

90   *City of God* 14.18 (Dods).

91   See *Faith, Hope, and Charity* 8.23ff. For particular discussions of concupiscence, see *On the Grace of Christ, and On Original Sin* 41; *The City of God* 14.20.

92   *On the Grace of Christ, and On Original Sin* 7f. See Peter J. Riga, "Created Grace in St. Augustine," *Augustinian Studies* 3 (1972), p. 115.

93 *City of God* 13.6 (Dods). See Ibid., 13.4; *Faith, Hope, and Charity* 14:48ff.; *City of God* 13.1; *On the Grace of Christ, and On Original Sin* 44. See also Gerald Bonner, *Augustine and Modern Research on Pelagianism*, p. 17; Godsey, p. 8.

94 *Confessions*, 2.2.4 (Chadwick). See *Faith, Hope, and Charity* 8.27ff.

95 Ibid., 7.18.25 (Chadwick).

96 Ibid., See *Faith, Hope, and Charity* 9.28ff.; Pelikan, p. 220f., ref. Rm 5:5; M. Cleary, "Augustine, Affectivity and Transforming Grace" in *Theology* (Jan./Feb. 1990), pp. 208-209: "Delight and love became key concepts in Augustine's understanding of the working of grace.... Ignorance of the crucial role of delight and love in the dynamics of grace and freedom only leads to a misunderstanding of the basics of Augustine's theology. Grace is not opposed to freedom, overriding it. Rather, true freedom of action is to be found in being supremely attracted to someone in such a way that love becomes so gradually unimpeded that nothing will hold us back; no alternatives, no matter how superficially attractive, can take the place of delighting in the presence of someone to whom we are naturally drawn, for we were created for him.... 'No one can come to me unless the Father who sent me draws him' (Jn 6:44)."

97 *Confessions* 10.22.32 (Chadwick).

98 See *Faith, Hope, and Charity* 13.46f. See Ibid., 5.10.18; 7.3.5; 8.5.10-11; 8.8.20-24; 9.1.1., for extended discussions of the will. See also Riga, p. 118.

99 See Ibid, pp. 51ff. See also Riga, p. 129.

100 *Confessions* 10.37. See Ibid., 13.16.21; 8.10.22; 8.7.13-8.14.

101 Bonner, pp. 1, 15.

102 See *Holy Virginity* 47.47. See also On *the Grace of Christ, and On Original Sin* 10ff.; *Free Choice of the Will* 1.15.107, 113-114; Cleary, pp. 204; Bonner, *Augustine and Modern Research on Pelagianism*, p. 18; Brown, *Augustine of Hippo*, p. 365; Riga, p. 114.

103 See *On the Grace of Christ, and On Original Sin* 2.12-14, for Augustine's argument against the following Pelagian tenet: As people sin by following Adam's example, so they are graced by following Christ's example; Bonner, *Augustine and Modern Research on Pelagianism* p. 30.

104 *Confessions* 1.7.11 (Chadwick). See *On the Grace of Christ, and On Original Sin* 2.44; Bonner, *Augustine and Modern Research on Pelagianism*, p. 30.

105 Ibid., 1.3.3 (Chadwick). See Ibid., 11.29.39; Cleary, p. 207.

106 Ibid., 2.1.1.

107 *On the Grace of Christ, and On Original Sin* 1.4 (NPNF, vol. 5).

108 Ibid., 1.4f. See Chadwick, *Augustine*, pp. 108f.

109 *Confessions* 1.7.11 (Chadwick). See Ibid., 4.15.25.

110 *On the Grace of Christ, and On Original Sin* 1.17.16 (NPNF I, vol. 5).

111 Ibid., 1.20.19 (NPNF I, vol. 5): "A man makes himself corrupt when he falls away from Him who is the unchanging good; for such a declension from Him is the origin of an evil will. Now this declension does not initiate some other corrupt nature, but it corrupts that which has already been created good. When this corruption, however, has been healed, no evil remains; for although nature no doubt had received an injury, yet nature was not itself to blame."

112 *Confessions* 1.20.31 (Chadwick).

113 *On the Grace of Christ, and On Original Sin* 1.8.7 (NPNF I, vol. 5).

114 Ibid., 1.28.27. See Chadwick, *Augustine*, p. 108f.; Patout J. Burns, "The Interpretation of Romans in the Pelagian controversy," *Augustinian Studies* 10 (1979), p. 45.

115 Ibid., ref Rm 8:10; 4:15; 7:7; 3:19-21.

116 Ibid., 1.31.30 (NPNF I, vol. 5): "Well, now, how is *that* grace which is not gratuitously conferred? How can it be grace, if it is given in payment of a debt? How can that be true which the apostle says, 'it is not of yourselves, but it is the gift of God; not of works, lest any man should boast' (Eph 2:8, 9); and again 'if it is of grace, then is it no more of works, otherwise grace is no more grace' (Rm 6:6).... Therefore, [Pelagius and Caelestius] attribute faith to free will in such a way as to make it appear that grace is rendered to faith not as a gratuitous gift, but as a debt — thus ceasing to be grace any longer... [these men] nowhere really acknowledge grace.... For that which God promises we do not ourselves bring about by our own choice or natural power, but He Himself affects it by grace."

117 *The Soliloquies* 1.3; 1.5, *emphases* added (NPNF I, vol. 7).

118 *On the Trinity* 1.12.13; *Confessions* 2.2.2. See *Free Choice of the Will* 1.15.106f.; 1.15.113; 1.16.114 (Benjamin and Hackstaff): "[There are] two kinds of men... those who pursue and love eternal things, and those who pursue and love temporal things." See also Gillette, p. 192f.

119 *On the Trinity* 8.8.12 (FC, vol. 45).

120 *On the Trinity* 3.7.11 (FC, vol. 45). See *Confessions* 2.2.2.

121 *Confessions* 4.1.1 (Chadwick). See Ibid., 2.2.2; *On the Trinity* 12.11.16; 8.7; Clark, p. 175, referring to *The Epistles of St. John* 7.8.

122 *Confessions* 4.12.18. See Clark, p. 51. 123.

123 *On the Trinity* 12.11.16 (FC, vol. 45).

124 *Christian Combat* 11.12 (FC, vol. 2).

125 *City of God* 21.26.

126 See Ph 3:13-15.

127 For a wider discussion of related themes, see *Free Choice of the Will* 1.15.105ff. See also Clark, pp. 46ff.

128 See Trape, p. 438: "Christian justification introduces already here on earth the restoration of the image of God which 'immortally imprinted in the immortal nature of the soul' (*On the Trinity* 14.4.6), sin had obscured although not destroyed (Ibid., 14.3.18; 15.8.14), the divine life of grace." See also *City of God* 27.3f.; *Free Choice of the Will* 1.12.85-87; 3.19.53; *Retractions*, 1.9.4. Clark, p. 68, summarizes Augustine's theological perspective of post-lapsarian freedom: "Freedom, like happiness, is the gift of God, but that to receive this gift man's consent is indispensable at all times. Man's part in the attainment of freedom today is to pray for divine help, to obey the law of his nature, and to allow Christ to liberate him through love."

129 *Confessions* 4.12.18 (Chadwick).

130 *On Christian Doctrine* 1.6 (NPNF I, vol. 2). See Gillette, p. 194; *Expositions on the Psalms* 103.1-4ff.; *Christian Combat* 11.12 (FC, vol. 2): "We have been shown to what a weakened state man has come by his own fault and how he is liberated from that state by divine assistance. The Son of God then assumed a human nature

and bore patiently all human misery. The healing power of this medicine for men is beyond all comprehension. For, what pride can be cured, if it is not cured by the humility of the Son of God?"

131 *Sermons on the Epistle of St. John* 251.6 (FC, vol. 38), ref. Phil. 3.13-15. See *Sermons on New Testament Lessons* 80.120.2f.; *Expositions on the Psalms* 103.1.4f.; Gillette, pp. 192ff.

132 *Christian Combat*, 11.12 (FC, vol. 2).

133 *Confessions* 9.2.3 (Chadwick). See *On the Trinity* 12.7.12; 14.4.6; 14.8.11; 14.14.18; 14.8.11. See *Confessions*, 9.4.8 (Chadwick): "'When I called upon You, You heard me, God of my righteousness; in tribulation You gave me enlargement. Have mercy on me, Lord, and hear my prayer' (Ps 4:2).... I was expressing the most intimate feeling of my mind with myself and to myself." See also Trape, p. 413.

134 *Free Choice of the Will* 2.16.169ff (Benjamin and Hackstaff): "Woe to the men who turn from Your light and cling complacently to their own darkness! When they turn their back to You, they are fixed in the work of the flesh, as in their own shadows; yet even there, they receive what delights them from the encompassing brightness of Your light (2.16.170). But love of the shadow causes the soul's eye to become too lazy and weak to endure the splendor of the sight of You. Besides, the more willingly and more indulgently a man follows and accepts something very weak, the more he becomes covered with darkness, and gradually he becomes unable to see what is supreme. He begins to think that some evil is deceiving him in his blindness, or attracts him in his poverty, or has captured and is torturing him. Yet he is really suffering deservedly because he has turned from the light of wisdom; what is just cannot be evil" (2.17.171).

135 *Confessions* 9.2.2 (Chadwick). See Ibid., 2.9.17; *Expositions on the Psalms* 4.9.

136 Ibid., 4.7.18 (Chadwick). See Ibid., 2.41.66; 2.9.17.

137 Gillette, p. 194, citing Augustine 1 John 4:19 in Augustine's *Epistle of John* 9.9. See *Confessions* 9.4.10.

138 *Confessions* 9.10.23 (Chadwick), *emphases* added. See footnote for debate about the meaning of this passage. Chadwick wonders: "Does Augustine imply that the ecstasy of Ostia was an anticipation of the beatific vision? Or does he mean the most divine part of the soul, most nearly akin to God, which analogy in Plotinus (5.1.3.4-6) might suggest? Elsewhere Augustine interprets 'the first fruits of the spirit' to mean the spirit of man, which would favor the latter view. The description of the vision at Ostia has affinities with Plotinus 5.1.2.14ff., a text also found congenial by St. Basil."

While the debate about Augustine's intentions is important, I would argue that the two meanings above are not opposed. Rather, if purity of heart and the vision of God are organically related, then the soul that approaches the perfections of God insofar as grace allows is, itself, an anticipation and reflection of the Beatific Vision.

139 *City of God* 11.28 (Dods).

140 *Confessions* 9.11.33.

141 *On the Trinity* 13.1.1; 13.2.5.

142 See *Confessions*, chapters 3, 4 ff.; *On the Trinity*, chapters 13ff. For faith and Scripture see *On Christian Doctrine* 2.9 (NPNF I, vol. 2): "Among the things that are plainly laid down in Scripture are to be found in all matters that concern faith and the manner of life."

143 *Confessions* 4.4.7 (Chadwick). Augustine adds, however, that God cannot be dismissed: "You were present, immediately at the back of those who flee from You, at once both 'God of vengeances' (Ps 93:1) and fount of mercies: You turn us to Yourself in wonderful ways."

144 *Confessions* 3.11.19 (Chadwick). See Ibid., 3.11.17,19 and 4.4.7; *City of God* 21.26; Clark, pp. 116f.

145 *Confessions* 5.9.17 (Chadwick).

146 See *Against Julian of Eclanum* 3.1.2; *Against Two Letters of the Pelagians* 3.8.24; 4.7.19; *On the Proceedings of Pelagius* 14.30; *On the Predestination of the Saints* 3.7; 4.8; *On the Gift of Perseverance* 21.55. See also Trape, p. 441.

147 *Admonition and Grace* 8.17 (FC, vol. 2).

148 *Confessions* 1.11.17 (Chadwick).

149 Ibid. (Chadwick).

150 *Christian Combat* 32.35 (FC, vol. 2).

151 *City of God* 21.15. See *Confessions* 1.1.1.

152 *On The Trinity* 14.1.3 (FC, vol. 45). See Pelikan: "[W]hile time could heal wounds, it did not necessarily cure vanity, which... only became worse with the increase of the years. (*Confessions* 7.1.1) Salvation, consequently, took place within time, but not by time. For the faith that attached itself to things eternal was itself a temporal phenomenon, 'dwelling within time in the hearts of believers' (*On the Trinity* 14.1.3) as the object of the faith was the Eternal who had appeared in time. In the call of God to faith, here within time, the historical time-as-sequence (*chronos*) could become the existential time-as-summons (*kairos*), which declared: 'Let it be done now!' (*Confessions* 11.24; *On Christian Doctrine* 3.36.54)."

153 *Concerning the Correction of the Donatists* 9.40 (NPNF I, vol. 4).

154 *Confessions* 4.4.7 (Chadwick). See *Sermon* 190.1.

155 Ibid., 2.3.5 (Chadwick).

156 *On the Trinity* 18.24 (FC, vol. 45).

157 *Confessions* 1.1.1. See *Free Choice of the Will* 1.2.12 (Benjamin and Hackstaff): "To hold God supreme is most truly the beginning of piety; and no one holds Him supreme who does not believe Him to be omnipotent and absolutely changeless." See also Gillette, pp. 192-193.

158 *On the Trinity* 1.1.1 (FC, vol. 45). See Gilson, p. 12: "Augustine does not try to show him the truth of Scripture, which teaches that God does exist. Only after he has obtained this *act of faith* in God's existence will he undertake to prove to the fool the rational character of his belief.... No facet of Augustine's philosophy escapes the *Credo ut intelligam* (I believe in order that I may understand), not even the proof for the existence of God."

159 *Expositions on the Psalms* 52.2; 13; 52. See Chadwick, *Confessions*, Introduction, p. xxiii; Gilson, p. 12.

160 Gilson, p. 30 on *Epistle* 120. See *Sermon* 43.3.4.

161 *Sermon* 190.2 (FC, vol. 38). See *Against Julian of Eclanum* 4.14.72; Clark, p. 131; Gilson, p. 31.

162 *On the Literal Interpretation of Genesis* 1.13.28. See *On The Trinity* 9.1.1; Gilson, p. 27: "[A]fter a depressing period of skepticism during which he was harrowed by

despair of ever finding truth, he discovered that faith held possession in perpetuity of the very truth his reason had been unable to grasp. In theory, then, it seems quite logical to start from reason in order to come to faith; in practice, however... the opposite method the better... better to believe in order to know."

163   Gilson, p. 36, footnotes 40; 41. See Ibid., p. 181 on Acts 15:9. See also *Letter* 137; 4; *Tractates on the Gospel of John* 27.6.7-9.

164   See Gilson, p. 31.

165   Gilson, p. 31. See *City of God* 21.2.

166   *On the Trinity* 8.1.2 (FC, vol. 45). See Ibid., 8.5.8; 15.2.2. See Pelikan, p. 56; Gilson, p. 28 defines the Augustinian understanding of belief as "a knowledge possessed by the mind, like any knowledge, and it differs from the latter only in its source." (See *Letter* 147.2.7) See Ibid., p. 27: "Belief is such a natural and necessary act of the mind that we cannot imagine a human life in which it does not occupy a very large place. Belief... is simply thought accompanied by assent." (See *On the Predestination of the Saints* 2.5)

167   *On the Trinity* 9.1.1 (FC, vol. 45). See *Sermon* 234.3; *On Christian Doctrine* 2.12; *Sermon* 212.1.

168   *Confessions* 13.12.13 (Chadwick). See *Free Choice of the Will* 2.2.18-19; 3.21.203. See also *On The Trinity* 8.5.8.

169   Ibid., 13.13.14. See Gilson, p. 12.

170   *Sermons on New Testament Lessons* 3.53.10-11; *Letter* 120.2.7f. See Gilson, p. 32.

171   Ibid. See *Sermon* 162A.2. See also Gillette, p. 183; Ac 15:9; Gal 5:6ff; 2 Cor 5:16ff; 1 Cor 13:1ff.

172   See *Against Faustus the Manichaean* 5.4; *On the Trinity* 18.24f.

173   Ibid., 11.17.28-29 (FC, vol. 45).

174   Ibid., 13.7.10 (FC, vol. 45).

175   *On the Trinity* 13.7.10 (FC, vol. 45). See Ibid., 1.10.21; 1.12.31; *On Christian Doctrine* 1.35-37 (NPNF I, vol. 2).

176   Ibid., 1.8.17 (FC, vol. 45), *emphases* added. See Ibid., 1.12.31.

177   *On the Merits and Forgiveness of Sins* 2.5. See *On the Trinity* 1.12.31; 1.8.17; 1.12.31.

178   *Confessions* 6.16.26. See *Sermon* 136C.2; *On the Trinity* 1.12.31; Gillette, p. 177.

179   Ibid., 7.1.1 (Chadwick). See Ibid., 7.1.2; 9.4.10.

180   Ibid., 9.9.10 (Chadwick).

181   Ibid. See Psalm 4.7.

182   See Gillette, p. 176, footnote 7 referencing Augustine's treatment of this concept in *Letter* 147.52-54 and *City of God* 22.29.

183   See *Our Lord's Sermon on the Mount* 2.13.45ff.; *On the Trinity* 1.2.4.; Gillette, pp. 176f.

184   See *Sermon* 88.5. See also Margaret Miles, "Vision: The Eye of the Body and the Eye of the Mind in Saint Augustine's *De trinitate and Confessions*" in *Journal of Religion* 63 (1983), pp. 125-42.

185   *Confessions* 13.19.24 (Chadwick).

186 *Sermon* 194.4 (FC, vol. 38).

187 See *Free Choice of the Will* 1.6.43; 3.5.61; 3.6.101; *On the Trinity* 10.9.10; *Confessions* 11.2.2; *On the Catholic and Manichaean Ways of Life* 7.11; *City of God* 22.29; *Sermon* 88.5; *Letter* 147.52ff.

188 *On the Catholic and Manichaean Ways of Life* 22.20f.; *On the Trinity* 10.5.7; 10.6.8; 10.7.9; 12.7.12. See Benjamin and Hackstaff, p. xxivf., Introduction to *Free Choice of the Will*.

189 *Free Choice of the Will* 2.19.200 (Benjamin and Hackstaff). See Ibid. 1.7.60; 10.5.7; 10.6.8; 10.7.9; *On the Trinity* 9.4.4; 10.5.7; *Confessions* 6.16.26.

190 *City of God* 11.2 (Dods), *emphasis* in the text. See *Free Choice of the* Will 1.2.11; *Confessions* 6.16.24f.; Gilson, p. 11, 17f.

191 *Confessions* 10.14.22 (Chadwick).

192 Ibid., 10.17.26 (Chadwick). See Ibid., 10.24.35. See also Pelikan, p. 67.

193 Ibid.

194 Ibid., 10.23.33 (Chadwick). See *On the Trinity* 15.4.5 (FC, vol. 45).

195 See *Free Choice of the Will* 2.15.39; 2.12.34; 2.12.35ff.; 2.14.38.

196 *On the Catholic and Manichaean Ways of Life* 22.41 (NPNF, vol. 4).

197 See *Free Choice of the Will* 1.11.77f.; 1.11.76ff.; 1.12.81ff.; 1.2.1.8ff.; 3.4.40; *On the Trinity* 14.9.12; *City of God* 14.19; *On the Catholic and Manichaean Ways of Life* 12.20f.; 13.22; 22.40ff; 23.42. See also Clark, p. 51.

198 *On the Trinity* 14.16.22, *emphasis* added (FC, vol. 45).

199 *On the Trinity* 9.5.8 (FC, vol. 45). See Ibid., 9.2.2.; 9.4.4ff.

200 Ibid., 9.4.7.

201 See *Free Choice of the Will* 1.1.1; 2.7.179; 3.13.133; 3.15.145; *City of God*; 5.10; 7.6; 12.6. See also Clark, pp. 6, 174.

202 *Admonition and Grace* 12.33-34 (FC, vol. 2).

203 *City of God* 12.8 (Dods). See Pelikan, p. 86: "It was necessary to recognize, [Augustine] insisted, 'that free will, naturally assigned by the Creator to our rational soul, is a middle power [*media vis*], one that can either incline toward faith or turn toward unbelief.' (*Spirit and the Letter* 33.58) Augustine's picture of Adam before the fall, therefore, described him as possessing not only a free will, but the superadded gift of divine grace. As a 'middle power,' free will could not by itself sustain him. 'God did not will even him to be without his grace, which he left in his free will; because free will is sufficient for evil, but is too little for good, unless it is aided by Omnipotent Good,' that is, by the grace of God.' (*Admonition and Grace* 11.31)."

204 *Admonition and Grace* 13.24 (FC, vol. 2). See *City of God* 12.6ff.*; Free Choice of the Will* 2.20.201; *Against Faustus the Manichaean* 22.22.

205 See *Free Choice of the Will* 1.24.99; 1.26.114; 2.1.6f.; 3.24.249f.; 3.25.255. See also *Confessions* 12.11.11; *City of God* 12.6.

206 *Admonition and Grace* 12.38 (FC, vol. 2). See Ibid., 12.38; *Against Two Letters of the Pelagians* 1.2.5.

207 *Free Choice of the Will* 3.16.155 (Benjamin and Hackstaff). See Ibid., 3.15.145.

208 See *On the Trinity* 8.3.4f.

209 *Free Choice of the Will* 1.13.97 (Benjamin and Hackstaff). See Ibid., 1.13.95; 1.12.83: "What is good will? A will by which we seek to live rightly and honorably and to come to the highest wisdom"; *Confessions* 7.4.6.

210 See *Tractates on the First Epistle of John* 9.9; *Confessions* 11.2.3; *Christian Combat* 11.12; *City of God* 21.26; *Free Choice of the Will* 1.13.95; 1.14.99.

211 Peter Brown, *The Body and Society* (New York: Columbia University Press, 1990), p. 399: Brown mentions Gregory of Nyssa, Jerome, and Ambrose. See also Pelikan, p. 76.

212 *On the Good of Marriage* 1.1; 8.8.

213 *City of God* 13.10. (Dods). See footnote 13: "Much of this paradoxical statement about death is taken from Seneca."

214 See *Freedom of the Will* 1.16.34; 1.10.20; 1.15.35; *City of God* 14.3.

215 *On the Trinity* 15.4.5 (FC, vol. 45). Augustine adds "the image of the body which is in the memory, the form thence impressed when the gaze of thought is turned to it, and the attention of the will which joins both together." See *Confessions* 3.6.10.

216 *Against the Basic Letter of the Manichees* 41.47 (NPNF I, vol. 4), *emphases* added. See footnote pointing to the Neo-Platonic influence on Augustine's thought.

217 *On the Literal Interpretation of Genesis* 7.28.38; 12.35.68. See *On Christian Doctrine* 1.24ff.

218 *On the Literal Interpretation of Genesis* 7.28.38; 12.35.68; *On Christian Doctrine* 1.24ff.; *Christian Combat* 6.6. (FC, vol. 2). See *City of God* 13.16; *On the Trinity* 8.3.4; *On the Catholic and Manichaean Ways of Life* 4.6; 5.7 (NPNF I, vol. 4): "The chief good of the body... is not bodily pleasure, not absence of pain, not strength, not beauty, not swiftness, or whatever else... but simply the soul. For all the things mentioned the soul supplies to the body by its presence, and, what is above them all, life.... Whether there is anything which goes before the soul itself, in following which the soul comes to the perfection of good of which it is capable in its own kind. If such a thing can be found... we must pronounce this to be... the chief good of man."

219 *On the Catholic and Manichaean Ways of Life* 21.38 (NPNF I, vol. 4). See *City of God* 14.3.

220 Ibid., 13.2.

221 *Christian Combat* 13.14 (FC, vol. 2). See *Admonition and Grace* 6.9; 13.24; See *Confessions* 10.35.56 (Chadwick): "In this immense jungle full of traps and dangers, see how many I have cut from my heart, as You have granted me to do, 'God of my salvation' (Ps 17:47; 37:23)." See also Ibid., 4.11.16; 10.25.54; 10.20.41f.; 12.11.13; *On the Trinity* 18.24.

222 *Free Choice of the Will* 3.20.193 (Benjamin and Hackstaff). See *On the Catholic and Manichaean Ways of Life* 4.6; 5.7. See Gilson, pp. 27f.

223 Ibid.

224 *City of God* 14.4.

225 *Free Choice of the Will* 2.16.161-63 (Benjamin and Hackstaff), *emphases* added. See *Confessions* 4.10.15 (Chadwick): "'O God of hosts, turn us and show us Your face, and we shall be safe' (Ps 79:8). For wherever the human soul turns itself, other than to You, it is fixed in sorrows, even if it is fixed upon beautiful things external to

You and external to itself, which would nevertheless be nothing if they did not have their being from You…. Let these transient things be the ground on which my soul praises You, 'God creator of all' (Ps 145:2)."

226   Ibid. See *On the Trinity* 34.9.14; 12.10.15.

227   *On the Merits and Forgiveness of Sins* 1.55. See *Confessions* 6.11.20; 6.12.22 (Chadwick), where Augustine speaks of his persistent fear of embracing continence: "I longed for the happy life, but was afraid of the place where it has its seat, and fled from it at the same time as I was seeking for it. I thought I would become very miserable if I were deprived of the embraces of a woman. I did not think the medicine of Your mercy could heal that infirmity because I had not tried it. I believed continence to be achieved by personal resources which I was not aware of possessing. I was so stupid as not to know that, as it is written (Ws 8:21), 'no one can be continent unless You grant it.' You would surely have granted it if my inward groaning had struck Your ears and with firm faith I had cast my care on You…. To a large extent what held me captive and tortured me was the habit of satisfying with vehement intensity an insatiable sexual desire."

228   Gillette, p. 175.

229   Ibid. See *On the Trinity* 4.18.24; 4.21.31. See also *On Free Choice of the Will* 1.13.89f.

230   *On the Trinity* 4.18.24 (FC, vol. 45). See Ibid., 4.21.31; *On Free Choice of the Will* 23.89ff.

231   See *On the Trinity* 11.5.8 (FC, vol. 45). Augustine explains how all souls strive to be like God; however, the sinful souls strive in a perverse way: "God has made all things exceedingly good (see Ec 39:21) precisely because He Himself is the highest good. Insofar, therefore, as anything is, it is good, that is, to that extent it bears some resemblance, though very remote, to the highest good; and if a natural likeness, then certainly right and well-ordered, but if a defective likeness, then certainly shameful and perverse. For even in their very sins souls are only striving for a certain likeness to God in their proud, perverted, and so to speak, servile liberty. Thus our first parents could not have been persuaded to sin if it had not been said to them: 'You shall be as gods' (Gn 3:5)."

232   *On the Trinity* 7.3.5.

233   Ibid., 8.4.6 (FC, vol. 45). See Gilson, p. 8. See also *On Christian Doctrine* 1.17.

234   *Confessions* 13.19.10 (Chadwick). See Ibid., 11.1.1; *Confessions* 13.9.10; See also Trape, pp. 423f.

235   Ibid. (Chadwick).

236   See Ibid., 8.3.7.

237   See Ibid., 7.16.22; 7.17.23.

238   See *Christian Combat* 7.8.

239   See *On the Trinity* 4.18.24; 4.21.31. *On the Catholic and Manichaean Ways of Life* 13.21. See also Gilson, p. 32; Trape, p. 414.

240   See *Against Julian of Eclanum*, Unfinished Work 4.29; 4, 69; Trape, p. 414. See also *On the Trinity* 9.8.18 (FC, vol. 45): "This word is conceived in love, whether it be the word of the creature or the word of the Creator, that is of a changeable nature or of the unchangeable truth. Therefore, it is conceived either by desire [*cupiditas*] or love [*caritas*]: not that the creature ought not to be loved, but if that love for

him is referred to the Creator, it will no longer be desire but love. For desire is then present when the creature is loved on account of himself. Then it does not help him who uses it, but corrupts him who enjoys it. Since the creature, therefore, is either equal or inferior to us, we must use the inferior for God and enjoy the equal, but in God.... But the word is born when that which is thought pleases us, either for the purpose of committing sin or of acting rightly. Love, therefore, as a means, joins our word with the mind from which it is born; and as a third it binds itself with them in an incorporeal embrace, without any confusion."

²⁴¹ *City of God* 11.28.

²⁴² *Confessions* 10.40.65 (Chadwick). See Ibid., 10.23.34; 10.40.65; *City of God* 21.28; Pelikan, p. 32

²⁴³ Ibid., 10.23.34 (Chadwick).

²⁴⁴ Ibid. (Chadwick).

²⁴⁵ *Free Choice of the Will* 3.25.262 (Benjamin and Hackstaff).

²⁴⁶ Ibid.

²⁴⁷ Ibid. See *City of God* 12.8; 15.22 on disordered love as the cause of evil. See also Pelikan, p. 32.

²⁴⁸ *Confessions* 10.36.59 (Chadwick).

²⁴⁹ Ibid. See Ibid., 1.22.31; 10.36.59.

²⁵⁰ Ibid., 12.10.10.

²⁵¹ *On Christian Doctrine* 1.17 (NPNF I, vol. 2).

²⁵² *Confessions* 13.8.9 (Chadwick). See Ibid., 1.22.31.

²⁵³ Ibid., 9.4.10 (Chadwick).

²⁵⁴ *Confessions* 10.6.9; 10.6.10 (Chadwick), *emphases* added.

²⁵⁵ Ibid., 9.1.1. See *Tractates on the First Epistle of John* 7.8. See also Clark, p. 175.

²⁵⁶ Ibid. See Clark, p. 176: "The reward of a created will that participates in the Divine Will is to communicate with God in friendship.... The union of God and man is accomplished by God's omnipotent love, through which He can enter into the inviolable intimacy of the human heart.... Generosity is the truest way that man can image God... a condition for the use of the divine largesse: Man must admit that he is drawing on the goodness of God (see *On the Trinity* 8.7)."

²⁵⁷ Ibid.

²⁵⁸ Ibid. 9.1.1 (Chadwick).

²⁵⁹ See *On the Trinity* 13.16.20 (see Augustine on Romans 8:28ff.). See also *Confessions* 8.12.29f.

²⁶⁰ *On the Trinity* 13.9.13 (FC, vol. 45). See Ibid., 9.12.17: "The truth itself has persuaded us that, as no Christian doubts, the Son is the Word of God, so the Holy Spirit is love."

²⁶¹ Ibid., 8.10.13 (FC, vol. 45).

²⁶² Ibid.

²⁶³ Ibid., 8.4.6.

²⁶⁴ See *On the Catholic and Manichaean Ways of Life* 13.23.

²⁶⁵ *On the Trinity* 8.4.6 (FC, vol. 45), *emphases* added.

[266] See *On the Catholic and Manichaean Ways of Life*; *Tractates on the Gospel of John* 110.17.4. See also Gilson, p. 32.

[267] *On Baptism against the Donatists* 1.11.16.

[268] See Ibid.; *Our Lord's Sermon on the Mount* 1.19.60; 1.20.62ff.

[269] *Sermon on the Mount* 1.19.62 (NPNF I, vol. 6). See Ibid., 1.19.60; 1.19.63; *On the Trinity* 2.17.28.

[270] *On the Catholic and Manichaean Ways of Life* 26.48 (NPNF I, vol. 4). See Ibid., 17.31.

[271] Ibid., 26.49 (NPNF, vol. 4).

[272] Ibid., 26.50 (NPNF I, vol. 50). See Ibid., 26.51; *Confessions* 10.37.61.

[273] Ibid. See *Admonition and Grace* 7.13; *On the Trinity* 13.16.20.

[274] *On the Trinity* 8.8.12 (FC, vol. 45). See Ibid., 8.9.13. See also *Confessions* 11.12.3f.

[275] *Sermon* 261.8 (FC, vol. 38). See *Against Faustus the Manichaean* 17.16; *On the Catholic and Manichaean Ways of Life* 30.62; Trape, pp. 424f.

[276] *Sermon* 261.9 (FC, vol. 38). See Gillette, p. 185: "Love then perfects faith both by propelling us longingly toward God and by overflowing into concrete acts of love towards our neighbors.... We ought to do good to others for the sake of their salvation, and not for the sake of our own temporal gain. The very act which is performed with the proper intention perfects the initial purity in the heart and reflects it to others: 'The heart... is purified by behavior, by mode of life, by chastity, holiness, love, and by the faith which works through love.... [It] is like a tree that has its roots in the heart; deeds, after all, only proceed from the root of the heart. If you plant greed there, thorns proceed from it; if you plant charity, fruits proceed from it.' (*Sermon* 91.5)"

[277] *Confessions* 11.17.28 (FC, vol. 45). See Ibid., 21.2.3f.

[278] See *Confessions* 11.12.8f.; 8.9.21f.; 1.5.5; *On the Trinity* 9.9.14; 13.7.10. See also Clark, pp. 78f., 116, 123.

[279] *Confessions* 1.12.85ff. See *On the Trinity* 9.9.14.

[280] *Confessions* 1.12.86 (Chadwick).

[281] Ibid., 1.12.87 (Chadwick).

[282] Ibid., 8.10.22 (Chadwick). See Ibid., 8.9.21; *Christian Combat* 7.7; *Our Lord's Sermon on the Mount* 2.14.48; Clark, p. 116.

[283] *On the Catholic and Manichaean Ways of Life* 13.22 (NPNF I, vol. 4)

[284] *Against Two Letters of the Pelagians* 1.2.5. See Gilson, p. 32.

[285] *Our Lord's Sermon on the Mount* 2.25.82 (ACW, vol. 5).

[286] *Our Lord's Sermon on the Mount* 1.3.10 (ACW, vol. 5). See Ibid., 2.25.82; *Sermons on New Testament Lessons* 3.53.1. See also Trape, p. 456: "[Augustine] emphasizes the assimilative faculty of love by which 'each person is like unto that which he loves' (*Tractates on the First Letter of John* 2, 14).... To this there can rightly be added that of Doctor of Humility, since he spoke of this virtue with the same insistence. In Augustine's judgment humility is inseparable from charity — for which it constitutes the foundation, the approach and the dwelling. It is humility which distinguishes the city of God from the city of this world. He describes the nature, roots and the fruit of humility. Its nature consists in recognizing ourselves for what we are. Its roots are, essentially, three: the metaphysical root or creation, because of

which we have our own accord only limits and thus error and sin; the theological root or gratuitousness of grace, by which even our merits are a gift of God, who forgives us even the sins we have not committed; and the Christological root or the teaching and example of Christ, who brought this virtue into the world. The fruits of humility are many but can likewise be reduced to three: fortitude, victory, magnanimity."

287 *On the Catholic and Manichaean Ways of Life* 6.9f.

288 *Our Lord's Sermon on the Mount* 1.5.13 (ACW, vol. 5).

289 Ibid., 3.53.14. See 1.12.40: "It is evident from these precepts that our entire striving is to be directed towards inward joys, to keep ourselves from seeking outward rewards and becoming conformed to this world and forfeiting the promise of a blessedness which is the more solid and enduring as it is interior, and by which God chose us 'to be made conformable to the image of His Son' (Rm 8:29)."

290 Ibid., 15.25 (NPNF I, vol. 4). See Ibid., 1.1.1; 1.18.55; 2.11.38; 2.25.82.

291 *Free Choice of the Will* 1.14.100 (Benjamin and Hackstaff).

292 Ibid., 1.14.101 (Benjamin and Hackstaff). See Ibid., 1.13.89ff.

293 Ibid., 1.13.92 (Benjamin and Hackstaff). See *Our Lord's Sermon on the Mount* 1.18.54.

294 *On the Trinity* 13.13.17 (FC, vol. 45). See *On the Catholic and Manichaean Ways of Life* 15.25; 16.26.

295 Augustine maintains integrality of virtue and grace for the attainment of happiness. See *On the Catholic and Manichaean Ways of Life* 5.10; 6.9. See also *On the Trinity* 4.15.20 (FC, vol. 45): "There are certain ones... who think themselves capable by their own strength of being purified, so as to see God and to inhere in God, whose very pride defiles them above all others."

296 *Our Lord's Sermon on the Mount* 1.2.8 (NPNF I, vol. 6). See McKenna, trans., *On the Trinity*, FC, vol. 45, Introduction xii-xiii: "The mind of St. Augustine was always centered on God; he sought Him everywhere, and when he came across something that would help to make God better known and loved, he did not hesitate to write about it, even though he had to depart for a time from his main theme."

297 See *Confessions* 7.17.24; *On the Trinity* 5.1.2; *On Christian Doctrine* 1.30; *Our Lord's Sermon on the Mount* 1.2.9; 2.16.53; *Free Choice of the Will* 2.19.193.

298 *Confessions* 3.8.16 (Chadwick). See *Our Lord's Sermon on the Mount* 1.3.10.

299 Ibid.

300 *Admonition and Grace* 9.24 (FC, vol. 2).

301 *Our Lord's Sermon on the Mount* 2.2.9 (ACW, vol. 5). See Ibid., 2.17.56. See also Gillette, p. 180.

302 *On Christian Doctrine* 1.30 (NPNF I, vol. 2). See *Confessions* 10.35.57; 10.36.58; 13.17.21 (Chadwick): "As the earth produces her fruit, so at Your command, the command of its Lord God, our soul yields works of mercy 'according to its kind' (Gn 1:12), loving our neighbor in the relief of physical necessities, 'having in itself seed according to its likeness.' Aware of our own infirmity we are moved to compassion...."

303 *On the Trinity* 8.7.10 (FC, vol. 45). See *On Christian Doctrine* 1.40; *Sermon* 301A.2; *Confessions* 13.21.30f.; Gillette, p. 184.

304 *On the Trinity* 12.13.21 (FC, vol. 45).

305 *Confessions* 11.12.28 (Chadwick).

306 Ibid., 13.21.29 (Chadwick).

307 *Sermons on New Testament Lessons* 3.53.12 (NPNF I, vol. 6).

308 See *Confessions* 11.2.3. See also *On the Catholic and Manichaean Ways of Life* 11.19.

309 *On the Catholic and Manichaean Ways of Life* 11.19 (NPNF I, vol. 4): "For that
     which we love God cannot die, except in not loving God; for death is not to love
     God, and that is when we prefer anything to Him in affection and pursuit.... An-
     gels do not separate us; for the mind cleaving to God is not inferior in strength to
     an angel. Virtue does not separate us; for if what is here called virtue is that which
     has power in this world, the mind cleaving to God is far above the whole world....
     Present troubles do not separate us; for we feel their burden less the closer we cling
     to Him from whom they try to separate us.... Height and depth do not separate
     us; for if the height and depth and knowledge are what is meant, I will rather not
     be inquisitive than be separated from God.... What place can remove me from His
     love, when He could not be all in every place unless He were contained in none?"

310 *On Christian Doctrine* 1.7 (NPNF I, vol. 2).

311 *Sermon* 259.1 (FC, vol. 38). See *On the Catholic and Manichaean Ways of Life*
     11.19.

312 *Sermon* 190.2 (FC, vol. 38).

313 See *City of God* 13.1ff; 14.14f.; *On the Grace of Christ, and On Original Sin* 20; *Con-
     fessions* 3.8.16. See Brown, *The Body and Society*, pp. 394ff. See *City of God* 13.1ff;
     14.14f.; 14.26 (Dods), *emphases* added: "As in Paradise there was no excessive heat
     or cold, so its inhabitants were exempt from the vicissitudes of fear and desire. No
     sadness of any kind was there, nor any foolish joy; *true gladness ceaselessly flowed
     from the presence of God, who was loved 'out of a pure heart, and a good conscience,
     and faith unfeigned'* (1 Tm 1:5). The honest love of husband and wife made a sure
     harmony between them. Body and spirit worked harmoniously together, and the
     commandment was kept without labor. No languor made their leisure wearisome;
     no sleepiness interrupted their desire to labor.... When sexual intercourse is spoken
     of now, it suggests to men's thoughts not such a placid obedience to the will as is
     conceivable in our first parents, but such violent acting of lust as they themselves
     have experienced."

314 *Holy Virginity* 6.6.

315 Ibid., 3.3. (FC, vol. 27). See Ibid., 4.4; *Sermon* 69.3; *On the Merits and Forgiveness
     of Sins and on Infant Baptism* 2.24.

316 Ibid., 4.4.

317 Ibid., 6.6 (FC, vol. 27).

318 Ibid., 3.3. (FC, vol. 27). See Ibid., 2.2.

319 *Holy Virginity* 2.2; 2.7; 5.5. See *Sermon* 188.3 (FC, vol. 38): "The birth of her
     omnipotent Son detracted in no way from the virginity of holy Mary, whom He
     Himself chose when He contemplated the assumption of the human nature. Fertil-
     ity is a blessing in marriage, but integrity in holiness is better. Therefore, the Man
     Christ who was able to furnish both prerogatives to His Mother (for He was God as
     well as Man) would never have granted to His Mother the blessing in which wives
     delight in such a way as to deprive her of the better gift for which virgins forego
     motherhood."

320 *Sermon* 192.2; *Holy Virginity* 3.3. See *Confessions* 8.11.27 (Chadwick): "Lady Continence… in no sense barren but 'the fruitful mother of children' (Ps 112:9), the joys born of You, Lord, her husband…. Why are you relying on yourself, only to find yourself unreliable? Cast yourself upon Him, do not be afraid. He will not withdraw Himself so that you fall. Make the leap without anxiety; He will catch you and heal you."

321 *Holy Virginity* 2.2 (FC, vol. 27). See 2.2; 8.8; 29.29; 36.37.

322 *Sermon* 191.2 (FC, vol. 38).

323 *Holy Virginity* 13.12 (FC, vol. 27). See Ibid., 8.8; 14.14; 15.15; 16.16; 21.21.

324 Ibid., 13.12 (FC, vol. 27).

325 *On the Good of Marriage* 10.10 (FC, vol. 27).

326 Ibid.

327 *Holy Virginity* 4.4. (FC, vol. 27).

328 Ibid., 37.37; 38.39 (FC, vol. 27). See also 41.42f.; 42.43; 48.48; *Retractions* 2.23.

329 Ibid., 32.32 (FC, vol. 27). See Ibid., 1.1.

330 Ibid. See Ibid., 2.2; 37.37.

331 See Ibid., 27.27 (FC, vol. 27): "The special delights of the virgins of Christ are not the same as those of nonvirgins, although these be Christ's. There are other delights for the others, but such delights for no others. Enter into these. Follow the lamb, because the flesh of the Lamb is also virginal. For He preserved in Himself in His manhood what He did not take away from His Mother in His conception and birth."

332 Ibid., 51.52 (FC, vol. 27). See Ibid., 31.31; *On the Trinity* 8.5.7.

333 Ibid., 36.37 (FC, vol. 27).

334 Ibid., 27.27 (FC, vol. 27).

335 See Ibid., 36.37; 27.27.

336 Ibid., 2.2 (FC, vol. 27).

337 Ibid., 6.6 (FC, vol. 27). See Ibid., 5.5; 11.11; 12.11; 37.37.

338 Ibid., 37.37 (FC, vol. 27), *emphases* added.

339 *Sermon* 121.3 (FC, vol. 38).

340 *Holy Virginity* 11.11 (FC, vol. 27). See Ibid., 5.5; 12.11.

341 *On the Good of Marriage* 29.29.; 23.31.

342 Ibid., 24.32 (FC, vol. 27).

343 Ibid., 19.22 (FC, vol. 27).

344 Ibid., 24.32 (FC, vol. 27). See Ibid., 21.25; 23.31; 24.32; 23.31; 29.29.

345 See Ibid., 21.25; 23.31; 24.32. See *On Christian Doctrine* 3.11ff.; *Holy Virginity* 192.2ff.; *City of God* 14.26.

346 Ibid.

347 *On the Good of Marriage* 21.31f.

348 Ibid., 21.26 (FC, vol. 27).

349 See *City of God* 1.18; *Confessions* 1.19.30; *On the Good of Marriage* 24.32.

350 *Confessions* 8.11.27 (Chadwick).

351 See *Holy Virginity.*, 21.26; 22.27; See also *City of God* 1.16ff.; *Sermon* 192.2; 205.5; *Confessions* 8.10.24.

352 *Confessions* 10.30.45 (Chadwick).

353 Ibid.

354 Ibid., 10.29.40 (Chadwick). See Ibid. 10.36.60.

355 Ibid., 11.31.41 (Chadwick).

356 *Christian Combat* 2.2 (FC, vol. 2).

357 See *Sermon* 192.2; *On the Good of Marriage* 19.22; 20.24; 24.31ff.

358 *On the Trinity* 14.19.25 (FC, vol. 45).

359 *On the Catholic and Manichaean Ways of Life* 16.29.

360 See *Confessions* 9.1.1.

361 Ibid., 8.1.1 (Chadwick), *emphasis* added.

362 Ibid., 1.6.9 (Chadwick).

363 *On the Catholic and Manichaean Ways of Life* 7.12 (NPNF, vol. 4); *On the Trinity* 13.1.1.

364 *Confessions* 10.2.4 (Chadwick).

365 *Admonition and Grace* 1.2; *City of God* 12.22; *Against Faustus the Manichaean* 36.40; *On the Trinity* 1.8.18.

366 *Confessions* 8.7.8 (Chadwick). See *On the Trinity* 1.8.8; *City of God* 12.22.

367 See *Sermon* 189.3; 233.4; *On the Trinity* 13.16.21; 13.17.22; *Confessions* 8.4.9; *Admonition and Grace* 12.35

368 *Confessions* 1.2.2; 1.3.3 (Chadwick).

369 *City of God* 21.26 (Dods).

370 *On Christian Doctrine* 1.16 (NPNF I, vol. 2).

371 *Expositions on the Psalms* 36.3.19. See *A Treatise Concerning the Correction of the Donatists* 9.42 (NPNF I, vol. 4): "[In] this world, no one is righteous by his own righteousness, that is, as though it were wrought by himself, and for himself; but as the Apostle says, 'According as God hath dealt to every man the measure of faith.... For as we have many members in one body, and all members have not the same office; so we, being many, are one body in Christ' (Rm 12:3-5). And according to this doctrine, no one can be righteous so long as he is separated from the unity of this body."

372 *Sermon* 243.2 (FC, vol. 38). See Ibid., 243.1; 244-245.

373 Ibid., *emphases* added.

374 Ibid.: The Church answers in the type of Mary Magdalene: "'I believed at the time when Jesus ascended to His Father.' What does 'I believed at that time' mean except 'I touched at that time'? Many earthly-minded persons believed that Christ was merely a Man; they did not discern the divinity which lay concealed in Him. They did not touch well because they did not believe well. Do you wish to touch well? Then discern Christ where He exists co-eternal with the Father and you have touched Him."

375 *On the Merits and Forgiveness of Sins* 1.34; 2.9. See Trape, p. 385.

376   *On the Trinity* 14.17.23 (FC, vol. 45). See *Sermon* 233.1; *On the Trinity* 14.17.23; *On the Merits and Forgiveness of Sins* 1.16; 2.9.

377   *City of God* 13.7 (Dods).

378   *Sermon* 235.2 (FC, vol. 38); ref. Lk. 24:13-31. See *On Baptism, against the Donatists* 3.18.3; *On Christian Doctrine* 1.18.

379   *Christian Combat* 13.15 (FC, vol. 2). See *Against the Basic Letter of the Manichees* 4.5; *City of God* 22.5; *Letter* 137.4ff; *On the Unity of the Church* 14.13ff; Trape, p. 404.

380   *On the Catholic and Manichaean Ways of Life* 30.62 (NPNF I, vol. 4).

381   *Sermon* 188.3; 192.2.

382   *On the Trinity* 1.1.3 (FC, vol. 45).

383   Ibid., 1.1.2 (FC, vol. 45).

384   See *Confessions* 11.2.3; *On the Catholic and Manichaean Ways of Life* 8.34; *Free Choice of the Will* 3.21.210f. See also Gilson, p. 33; Trape, p. 425; Pelikan, p. 57.

385   *Free Choice of the Will* 21.210 (Benjamin and Hackstaff). See *On the Trinity* 4.1.2; *City of God* 1.15.

386   *On Christian Doctrine* 3.10 (NPNF I, vol. 2).

387   See *Exposition on the Psalms* 90.2.1; *Letter* 28.3.3; 82.1.3; *City of God* 11.3; *Against Faustus the Manichaean* 11.5; *On the Catholic and Manichaean Ways of Life* 18.34. See also *Harmony of the Gospels*; Trape, p. 427f.

388   *City of God* 7.31; 10.1; *Our Lord's Sermon on the Mount* 2.3.11.

389   See *On Nature and Grace* 43.50; *Our Lord's Sermon on the Mount* 2.3.4; *Sermon* 80.7; *Letter* 130.17. See also Trape, p. 457.

390   *Sermon* 210.1 (FC, vol. 38). See Ibid., 210.5.

391   *City of God* 5.10. See *Admonition and Grace* 6.10 (FC, vol. 2): "'Be ye, therefore holy, because I am holy' (Lv 19:2). Our prayer and petition is that we who were sanctified in Baptism may persevere in what we have begun to be. The thought of the glorious martyr is that in these words the Christian faithful daily pray for perseverance in what they have begun to be.... Whoever begs of the Lord perseverance in good, confesses that this perseverance is His gift."

392   *Our Lord's Sermon on the Mount* 2.3.14 (ACW, vol. 5), *emphases* added.

393   Ibid., 2.3.11 (ACW, vol. 5).

394   Ibid.

395   Ibid., 6.56.1ff. See *Admonition and Grace* 6.10. See also Gillette, p. 183.

396   *Sermon* 207.2 (FC, vol. 38).

397   *On the Use of Fasting* 2-5 (Augustine devoted this brief work to fasting and oneness); *Sermon* 61.12; 205.2; 206.2; 207.1f.; 236.2f.; *Our Lord's Sermon on the Mount* 2.3.14; 2.12.42. See Gillette, pp. 187ff.

398   *Our Lord's Sermon on the Mount* 2.3.14. See *Free Choice of the Will* 3.22.223 (Benjamin and Hackstaff): "The dearer the Source of its being becomes the soul, the more firmly does the soul rest in Him, and the more richly does it delight in His eternity." See also the sources cited in the previous endnote.

399   *Sermon* 236.2f. (FC, vol. 38).

[400] *Our Lord's Sermon on the Mount* 2.5.17 (ACW, vol. 5). See also Ibid., 2.5.18; 6.56.1ff.; 2.12.43: "[We ought to do others] good for their eternal salvation.... For the end of the commandment is 'charity out of a pure heart, and a good conscience, and of faith unfeigned' (1 Tm 1:5)."

[401] *On the Trinity* 1.12.31 (FC, vol. 45), *emphases* added.

[402] *On the Catholic and Manichaean Ways of Life* 3.4 (NPNF I, vol. 4). See *Free Choice of the Will* 1.13.98f

[403] *On the Catholic and Manichaean Ways of Life* 8.13 (NPNF I, vol. 4). See Mt 2:37; Rm 8:28, 35).

[404] *Our Lord's Sermon on the Mount* 2.13.45 (NPNF I, vol., 6).

[405] See *The Rule of St. Augustine* (www.geocities.com/Athens/1534/ruleaug.html.). See also *Sermon* 2.13.45; Gilson, pp. 4f.

[406] *On Christian Doctrine* 1.4 (NPNF I, vol. 2). See also Ibid., 1.5; *Freedom of the Will* 3.7.70f.; *Confessions* 5.2.2.

[407] *On Christian Doctrine* 1.4 (NPNF I, vol. 2).

[408] Ibid.

[409] *Confessions* 4.13.20 (Chadwick).

[410] Ibid.

[411] *Confessions* 5.2.2

[412] *Sermon* 261.5 (FC, vol. 38).

[413] *Our Lord's Sermon on the Mount* 1.4.11f.; 2.13.44; *Sermon* 261.1; 261.5f.; *Sermons from New Testament Lessons* 3.53.6.

[414] *Confessions* 12.11.12 (Chadwick).

[415] *Free Choice of the Will* 2.13.141 (Benjamin and Hackstaff). See *On the Catholic and Manichaean Ways of Life* 15.47.

[416] Gilson, p. 8. See *On the Happy Life* 4.34.

[417] *Free Choice of the Will* 1.13.98 (Benjamin and Hackstaff). See Ibid., 2.13.137.

[418] Ibid., 2.16.168 (Benjamin and Hackstaff). See Ibid., 2.13.141; *On the Morals of the Catholic Church* 1.2.3; 8.13; *Sermons on New Testament Lessons* 3.53.7. See also Pablo Goni, *La resurreccion de la carne segun San Augustin* (Washington, DC: Catholic University of America, 1961), p. 121. See also Gilson, p. 34.

[419] *Sermons on New Testament Lessons* 3.53.7 (NPNF I, vol. 6).

[420] *On the Trinity* 3.2.8 (FC, vol. 45).

[421] Ibid.

[422] *Free Choice of the Will* 2.9.103.

[423] See Ibid., 2.9.102f.; *On the Trinity* 4.2.4; *Tractates on the Gospel of John* 8.6; *Confessions* 13.1.1f. See Trape p. 422.

[424] See *On the Catholic and Manichaean Ways of* Life 4.6ff.; *Sermon* 261.4; *Admonition and Grace* 6.10.

[425] See *Confessions* 8.4.5. *On the Trinity* 4.2.4; *Tractates on the Gospel of John* 48:9; *Explanations of the Letter to the Galations* 30.6; *Expositions on the Psalms* 49.1.1.; *Sermon* 166.4; *Letter* 140.2:10-12. See Jeffrey Finch, *Sanctity as Participation in the*

Divine Nature according to the Ante-Nicene Eastern Fathers, Considered in the Light of Palamism (Doctoral Dissertation: Drew University, May 2002), pp. 3ff.; Gerald Bonner, "Augustine's Conception of Deification," *Journal of Theological Studies* 37, no. 2 (1986), pp. 369ff.

426 *On the Trinity* 1.12.28 (FC, vol. 45).

427 *On the Merits and Forgiveness of Sins* 1.7 (NPNF I, vol. 5). See *On Nature and Grace* 24.26); *City of God* 13.4; 20.17; *Sermon* 205.1f.; *Free Choice of the Will* 3.20.195. See also *Sermon* 205.2 (FC, vol. 38): "O Christian, if you do not wish to sink into the mire of this earth, do not come down from the cross."

428 *City of God* 13.4 (Dods). See Ibid., 13.6; 13.8. See also Pelikan, pp. 33, 87.

429 *City of God* 7.31 (Dods).

430 *Sermons on New Testament Lessons* 3.53.6 (NPNF, vol. 5). See *On the Merits and Forgiveness of Sin* 1.7; *Our Lord's Sermon on the Mount* 2.5.17; *On the Trinity* 13.16.20; *Sermon* 261.4. See also Gillette, p. 182.

431 *On the Catholic and Manichaean Ways of Life* 11.18 (NPNF I, vol. 4).

432 *Sermon* 251.6, ref. Lk 10:38-41.

433 See *City of God* 19-30; *On the Literal Interpretation of Genesis* 7:27; *Sermon* 243.9. See also Clark, p. 52; Trape, pp. 422f.

434 *On the Trinity* 1.8.16 (FC, vol. 45). See *Admonition and Grace* 6.10 ref. to Ph 1:3 and Jude 2:4; *Against Faustus the Manichaean* 26.2.

435 *City of God* 19.20 (Dods). See *On the Catholic and Manichaean Ways of* Life 11.19; *City of God* 19.24; *Confessions* 2.1.1; Trape 458f.

436 *Sermons on New Testament Lessons* 3.53.16 (NPNF I, vol. 5). See *Sermon* 1.3.10; *City of God* 19.27.

437 *On the Trinity* 1.12.30 (FC, vol. 45).

438 *City of God* 22.25.

439 Ibid., 21.24.

440 *On the Trinity* 14.14.20 (FC, vol. 45).

441 *Confessions* 13.15.18 (Chadwick). See *On the Trinity* 14.18.24 (FC, vol. 45): "The Apostle John says: 'Dearly beloved, now we are the children of God, and it has not yet appeared what we shall be. But we know that, when He appears, we shall be like to Him, for we shall see Him just as He is' (1 Jn 3:2). Hence, it is clear that the full likeness to God will then be realized in this image of God when it shall receive the full vision of Him."

442 See *City of God* 22.29. See also Gilson, p. 7.

443 Ibid., 22.30 (Dods). See *Sermon* 243.4; *Faith, Hope, and Charity* 23.90.

444 Ibid.

445 *City of God* 22:30 (Dods). See Ibid., 29.27; *Faith, Hope, and Charity* 299.11.

446 *Sermon* 231.5; 233.1.

447 *On Christian Doctrine* 1.38 (NPNF I, vol. 3). See *Sermon* 231.5; 233.1.

448 Trape, p. 408 ref. to *On the Trinity* 5.2.3 and *City of God* 11.10.1.

449 *Sermon* 2.5.21. See Ibid., 2.6.20; *Literal Interpretation of Genesis* 4.6.12; 12.28.56.

450 *Sermon* 259.2 (FC, vol. 38). See *Faith, Hope, and Charity* 29:11ff.; 31.11.

[451] Ibid., 243.4.

[452] *Faith, Hope, and Charity* 23:84ff.; 23.90; *City of God* 22.12; 22.17; 22.20; *Sermon* 243.5ff.

[453] *City of God* 22.19 (Dods).

ST PAULS

This book was produced by ST PAULS/Alba House, the Society of St. Paul, an international religious congregation of priests and brothers dedicated to serving the Church through the communications media.

For information regarding this and associated ministries of the Pauline Family of Congregations, write to the Vocation Director, Society of St. Paul, 2187 Victory Blvd., Staten Island, New York 10314-6603. Phone (718) 982-5709; or E-mail: vocation@stpauls.us or check our internet site, www.vocationoffice.org